HIT LIST

FOR YOUNG ADULTS 2

Frequently Challenged Books

Teri S. Lesesne
and
Rosemary Chance

for the

Young Adult Library Services Association
of the
American Library Association

With a Foreword by
Chris Crutcher

American Library Association
Chicago and London
2002

LAKE COUNTY PUBLIC LIBRARY

While extensive effort has gone into ensuring the reliability of
information appearing in this book, the publisher makes no
warranty, express or implied, on the accuracy or reliability of
the information, and does not assume and hereby disclaims any
liability to any person for any loss or damage caused by errors
or omissions in this publication.

Printed on 50-pound white offset, a pH-neutral stock, and
bound in 10-point coated cover stock by McNaughton & Gunn

The paper used in this publication meets the minimum require-
ments of American National Standard for Information
Sciences—Permanence of Paper for Printed Library Materials,
ANSI Z39.48-1992. ∞

Library of Congress Cataloging-in-Publication Data

Lesesne, Teri S.
    Hit list for young adults 2 : frequently challenged books /
by Teri S. Lesesne, Rosemary Chance for the Young Adult
Library Services Association (YALSA) ; with a foreword by
Chris Crutcher.
      p. cm.
    Continues: Hit list : frequently challenged books for young
adults / prepared by the Intellectual Freedom Committee of the
Young Adult Library Services Association.
    Includes bibliographical references.
    ISBN 0-8389-0835-7
    1. Challenged books—United States—Bibliography.
2. Young adult literature, American—Bibliography.
I. Chance, Rosemary. II. Young Adult Library Services
Association. III. Hit list. IV. Title.

Z1019 .L48 2002
098'.1'0973—dc21   2002005749

Printed in the United States of America

06   05   04   03   02   5   4   3   2   1

CONTENTS

FOREWORD

BY CHRIS CRUTCHER

I have made peace with myself about censorship. I did it this way: I quit caring. Hey, people have been telling me to shut up all my life, and it's never worked before. My latest serious thoughts about interacting on the subject occurred only a month or so ago. The principal of a school in the Midwest e-mailed me and asked if I would reply to a challenge of several of my books by a small number of parents in his high school. He was a former English teacher and a fan of my work. His school district was conservative, and when the parents challenged the books with the intent of having them removed from the library, the school immediately compromised and offered to have them put on a restricted list. The principal and I e-mailed back and forth because my schedule might possibly allow me to be in his area on the night of the school board meeting, and he invited me to come and present my case. I was raring to go, but in the end my schedule was off by a day. When I sat down to draft a letter to the parents and the school board, a thought occurred that caused me to shut down my computer. *The minute those few parents complained, the school was willing to put the books on a restricted list to avoid the fight.* Sorry folks, but at that moment you validated the parents' point of view. You didn't stand up for intellectual freedom. So I mailed a letter stating what I stated above: I don't care.

When people want a book censored—be it mine or anyone else's—for "bad language," I can barely get up enough energy to address it. That language is spoken in the halls of every school, public and private, in the United States of America. It is in the movies and on television. When we censor it we give it more power than it has a right to. That's it. Putting the word "fuck" into a story is simply not a moral issue. And when we start that fight, we look foolish, trying to control something that is uncontrollable. It's just as easy to run across it and say "I don't like that," and have a dialogue about why not, as it is to try to shield it from our children's eyes, and we don't have to lose face.

When I worked as a child and family therapist at the Spokane Mental Health Center in the 1980s, we worked with a four-year-old mixed race girl I'll call Lisa, who had been removed from her family by Child Protective Services—along with her two Caucasian half-brothers—because they were discovered living in a U-Haul trailer. Her stepfather worked for the carnival and the family traveled in the trailer. Our program included individual, group, and family sessions, and we discovered early on that the stepfather was a vocal racist who held great anger at his wife for having "fucked a nigger" and much of his wrath ended up directed at Lisa—his constant reminder—at the end of every parental fight.

Despite living her life in a war zone, Lisa was one of the most physically attractive four-year-olds you'd ever want to meet. She was all muscle and gristle with a wide infectious smile and sparkling eyes. When an adult she didn't know came into the room, a parent or a practicum student or a newly hired therapist, Lisa would routinely plant herself in that person's path, smile, and extend her arms. It was almost impossible not to pick her up. When you raised her to eye level, she'd smile even wider and say "fuckerbitch," and what you did next wrote you in or out of her life forever. If you scolded her, or rejected her, she wrote you *off*. She would not sit at your table to eat, she would not allow you to read her a story, she would step around you as if you were furniture. If, on the other hand, you passed it off, or engaged it, or even distracted her attention to something else, she was *yours*. That was early in my career and I was lucky enough to have a real play therapist coaching me when Lisa looked me in the eye and cut loose with her little gem. Later the therapist said, "She was just seeing if you are safe." I was in the honored position of working with the kids three days a week and the parents two, and the next day Lisa's mom and stepdad got into a vicious argument during a group session and guess which words they screamed at each other in the heat of their fight? He was "fucker" and she was a "bitch." It didn't take a lot longer to understand that nearly all their fights ended with stepdad reminding mom what a nasty act she had had to perform, and with whom, to get Lisa in the first place, and it didn't take much imagination to know who ended up in the eye of the hurricane when that fight occurred unmonitored in the home.

Brilliant, if you think about it. Lisa used the two most dangerous words she knew; the words she heard before the walls caved in on her, to tell her whether or not adults were safe.

Now, I could tell that story and make up a word, or use some other combination, to make it more palatable, but the story would lose something: authenticity. There is a certain respect for Lisa and for the story to tell it as it happened. Also, as an adult working with Lisa, trying to help her bring the interior and the exterior of her life into congruence, I would *never* take that language away from her simply because sensitive people might be offended. Not without helping her find some text that would work equally as well. And if I wouldn't take it from her, I wouldn't take it from any character I might create who may have lived a life in the same war zone as Lisa. There is something respectful about telling the truth in its native tongue.

Recently I watched a rerun of a Barbara Walters interview of Eddie Murphy, one that took place back when Eddie was doing his one-hour comedy specials and had just finished the full-length feature *Eddie Murphy Raw,* which definitely *was* raw. Barbara leaned forward in that sincere, concerned manner she has, and said something to the effect of, "Eddie, you're a funny man, a comic genius. Why do you have to use the *language?*" and without missing a beat, Eddie said, "I don't *have* to use it. I just use it." He went on to explain that it is the language he grew up with, the language of the humor of that type of comedy. He was telling her about a small truth. And the fact is, if you don't spend your energy being offended, it's funny as hell, at least to a certain audience. If you don't like it, turn it off.

I don't pretend to have the persuasive powers to change the minds of the censors. There will always be people who believe it is their "moral" duty to watch over all of us rather than simply watch over themselves. What I wish they understood is this: Every time we adults show kids we are afraid of something that is offensive to us, we take ourselves off that short list of people to turn to in a true crisis. I received a letter from a middle school student not too long ago, chastising me for using the language I used in *Staying Fat for Sarah Byrnes,* and for the stances some of my characters took on the issues of religion and abortion. She told me that her mother had taken one look at the book and forbidden her to read it, but that her mother thought it was a good idea for her to write and let me know that I was offending children as well as adults. I didn't jump on the obvious issue, that the kid was slapping me upside the head for a book she hadn't read. What bothered me more was that *now,* while the girl was still young and still safely under her mother's control, all that was fine. They were united and it strengthened their bond, and that is well and good. And I *mean* that. It is well and good. The problem comes when this girl moves into adolescence, into that developmentally correct place of "pushing away" to become her own person; when she is titillated by sexual or "radical" ideas and becomes confused by the conflicting thoughts swirling in her head. Who is she going to turn to then? Who is she going to turn to when she knows her mother's views on the issues she has questions about are so rigid? When she knows she is going to disappoint her mother by questioning? Wouldn't it be *so* much smarter for her mom to entertain dialogue about the issues brought up in *Sarah Byrnes,* and discover the details of her daughter's confusion, and tell her how she came to her own conclusions? Is it *really* smart to keep our children ignorant? And what is this girl going to do if, God forbid, she makes a mistake out of curiosity and becomes pregnant? Who does she turn to then?

With any luck, she'll turn to me, or someone like me; not in my capacity as a trashy-mouthed writer, but in that of a child and family therapist. And I, or that person like me, will do his or her best to help this girl understand that she is not dirty, she is not immoral, she is not ruined. We will do our best to help her recover some self-esteem and muster some problem-solving skills to get through her crisis. In the best of worlds we will also sit down with her parents, in and out of her presence, and see if we can restructure some of their thinking about the difference between making grave mistakes and ruining a life.

I have heard a thousand times, "If you bring them up right, those kinds of things won't happen." That isn't true, folks. It just isn't. And you will betray yourselves and your children thinking and saying that. And you will also break your own hearts.

The battle about censorship may seem simple: a conflict between two ways of thinking about child development and learning. But it's way more than that.

I believe it was Kurt Vonnegut who once said that the problem with standing against censorship was with some of the trash you appeared to be standing *for*. But the operative word there is *appeared*. Being against censorship doesn't mean you don't think there is a lot of trash out there or that there is a lot of material you'd simply ignore if you get the chance. Being against censorship, in my opinion, is more about respect; not respect for the material, but respect for humans and their abilities to make decisions, and find quality in books and movies and television, and have intelligent discussions.

In the end, it's simply hard to see how we can protect people by keeping them ignorant.

INTRODUCTION

To paraphrase Charles Dickens, it is the best of times and the worst of times in the field of young adult literature. It is the best of all possible times because in the past ten years or so, young adult literature seems to have undergone a renaissance. Pundits of the 1980s had all but declared it dead. Teenagers had moved on to reading adult books; young adult literature now lacked the quality which it had enjoyed in its nascence. In short, why bother publishing books for this audience? However, before the patient could be officially declared dead, new life was breathed into the art form. Suddenly, there was renewed interest in the books and authors in the field. Newbery Awards were presented to young adult books and authors with increasing regularity. The Young Adult Library Services Association (YALSA) of the American Library Association (ALA) pioneered the first award in the field of young adult literature, the Michael L. Printz Award. Publishing houses began to extend the audience for young adult literature by publishing grittier and edgier books for older teens. Young adult literature, it seemed, was not only alive: it was thriving. In one sense, then, we are enjoying the best of times.

However, with renewed vigor comes renewed scrutiny, it seems. Never before has young adult literature been under such ferocious attack from censors. Between 1990 and 2000, 6,364 challenges were reported to or recorded by the ALA's Office for Intellectual Freedom (OIF; see the ALA OIF web site at http://www.ala.org/bbooks/challeng.html#backgroundinformation for details). Many challenges involved the young adult titles included in this edition. A brief survey by category indicates the growth in such challenges:

1,607 challenges to "sexually explicit" material (up 161 since 1999)

1,427 challenges to material considered to use "offensive language" (up 165 since 1999)

1,256 challenges to material considered "unsuited to age group" (up 89 since 1999)

842 challenges to material with an "occult theme or promoting the occult or satanism" (up 69 since 1999)

737 challenges to material considered to be "violent" (up 107 since 1999)

515 challenges to material with a homosexual theme or "promoting homosexuality" (up 18 since 1999)

419 challenges to material "promoting a religious viewpoint" (up 22 since 1999)

The large majority of the challenges were to material in schools or school libraries and were brought by parents.

Who, then, is the audience for this new edition of *Hit List?* Basically, anyone who has an interest in the field of young adult literature, or who works with adolescents in school or library settings, or who is interested in the preservation of the freedom to read will find something of value within the pages of this book. Public and school librarians will find this book helpful in the preparation of materials in defense of challenged books. Likewise, teachers and administrators can use this book to deal with challenges that might arise in relation to the books discussed here. Students seeking information about censorship will find this book useful. The material in this book might also be helpful for those conducting research into censorship.

This book was first published by YALSA in 1989, right at the beginning of the new golden age in young adult literature. The leaders of YALSA immediately saw the need for a tool to assist librarians, teachers, and other supporters of young adult literature who face censorship challenges, a guide that would provide a starting point in their defense of the materials being challenged. The second book entitled *Hit List* was published by ALA Editions in 1996 and was a best-seller because it provided such information. This new edition continues to provide the same type of information. Within the pages of this book, readers will find chapters focusing on twenty books read by teenagers. Some of the titles included here have appeared in previous editions of *Hit List* (such as *Fallen Angels, The Chocolate War,* and *I Know Why the Caged Bird Sings*), while others are new to this edition (including *Speak, Shade's Children,* and *The Perks of Being a Wallflower*). Many of the books appear on the top 10 and top 100 lists of banned books. Others, however, are relatively new additions to the list of challenged books. We decided to focus more intently on works written especially for the teen reader rather than on those classics often studied as part of the school curriculum. Most of the books included in this edition, then, are contemporary works written for and read by young adults.

Readers will also note some other changes in this edition of *Hit List.* As editors, we decided to focus on only one book by an author. So even though Robert Cormier, Chris Crutcher, and Judy Blume (among other authors) have several books on the banned book list, we focus on *The Chocolate War, Athletic Shorts,* and *Forever,* respectively. The chapters on these novels can serve as models for developing materials with which to defend other books by Cormier, Crutcher, Blume, and other authors that have been challenged. Likewise, we hope that the format and content of the chapters can serve as a framework for new materials which may be challenged after this edition is published.

The format of each chapter has been changed a bit from previous editions as well. Each chapter begins with a detailed summary of the contents of the book. Following the summary are listings of articles about the book and its author, awards and prizes the book or author have won, and other books written about the book or its author. These are followed by a listing of challenges to that book filed with the ALA's Office for Intellectual Freedom through mid-2001. Most of these challenges have been reported in one of three sources: *100 Banned Books: Censorship Histories of World Literature,* by Karolides, Bald, and Sova; *Limiting What Students Shall Read: Books and Other Learning Materials in Our Public Schools: How They Are Selected and How They Are Removed,* a report sponsored by the Association of American Publishers in 1981; and the *Newsletter on Intellectual Freedom,* edited by Judith Krug and published by the OIF. After the challenge listings, readers are provided with information about online resources for the book or author and a list of reviews of the book.

All of the sections are intended to provide as much information as possible for librarians, teachers, and other professionals who are preparing materials to defend against a challenge. Please note, though, that these resources are not comprehensive; new reviews, new articles, new challenges and resources appear daily in print and online. The editors have therefore included some suggestions for updating resources in the appendixes of this book.

We would like to thank the following people for their invaluable assistance in the preparation of this book. First, the Publications Committee of YALSA deserves thanks for suggesting this new edition of *Hit List,* as well as for suggesting some of the changes readers will note in this edition. Thanks to Linda Waddle, who was the Deputy Executive Director of YALSA during the preparation of the book. Thanks also go to Beverley Becker of the Office for Intellectual Freedom, who helped us coordinate our efforts and provided us with up-to-date materials about challenges. Karen Young of ALA Editions also provided guidance during the writing of this book. We thank her for her helpful suggestions. Finally, we would like to thank Chris Crutcher for taking time from his schedule to write the foreword to this book. We felt it was important for readers to hear from one of the warriors on the censorship battlefield. Thanks, Chris, for your words.

We hope this new edition of *Hit List* will assist all of you in your defense of books. Censorship tries to erect walls to keep readers out of so-called dangerous books. *Hit List* exists to break down those walls, to keep books accessible to all.

Editors' Note

Each year the Office for Intellectual Freedom of the ALA receives hundreds of messages about challenges to intellectual freedom. All challenges reported directly to the OIF are kept confidential. Only challenges reported in the media, primarily in newspapers, are discussed and documented in the *Newsletter on*

Intellectual Freedom. What does that mean for you and for this book? It means that you can get help from the ALA without publicizing a challenge, and it means that there are many more challenges reported to the OIF than the ones you see documented in this edition of *Hit List*.

Documentation for the challenges listed in this edition of *Hit List* comes primarily from the following three sources:

Karolides, N. J., M. Bald, and D. B. Sova. *100 Banned Books: Censorship Histories of World Literature.* New York: Checkmark Books, 1999.

Limiting What Students Shall Read: Books and Other Learning Materials in Our Public Schools: How They Are Selected and How They Are Removed. Report on a survey sponsored by the Association of American Publishers, the American Library Association, and the Association for Supervision and Curriculum Development. Washington, D.C.: Association of American Publishers, 1981.

Newsletter on Intellectual Freedom. Edited by Judith F. Krug. Chicago: American Library Association, Intellectual Freedom Committee, published bimonthly.

Edited by MARION DANE BAUER

Am I Blue? Coming Out from the Silence

New York: HarperCollins, 1994

This collection of short stories by noted young adult authors features gay and lesbian characters. The stories are sometimes funny, sometimes poignant, and occasionally bittersweet. All deal with coming-of-age issues in the lives of teen characters. Though the main characters may be gay or lesbian, many of the issues they face will resonate with all readers.

The title story, "Am I Blue?" by Bruce Coville, opens with Vince, who is accused of being gay, being roughed up by another young man. Vince's fairy godfather appears and grants Vince three wishes. The second of Vince's wishes is to have anyone who is gay turn blue. Vince also wishes that the bully who beat him for even appearing to be gay should be turned blue as well. The fairy godfather returns to let Vince know he has one more wish coming, since the bully who insinuated that Vince was gay is already a nice shade of blue.

In "We Might as Well All Be Strangers," M. E. Kerr shares the story of Alison and her grandmother. On a visit to her grandmother, Alison reveals that she is a lesbian. Alison's grandmother, in response, tells her of a visit she made as a schoolgirl to the home of one of her friends. Her friend lived in Germany at the time when Hitler was gaining power. Alison's grandmother was confronted with anti-Semitic remarks from some of the people she encountered in Germany.

She tells Alison that anti-Semitic and anti-homosexual sentiments have a lot in common. Alison's mother rejects this argument and finds the comparison of Jews and gays odious.

Francesca Lia Block's "Winnie and Tommy" deals with two young friends after high school graduation. The two have been friends and were even linked romantically at school. Tommy is gay and wants to remain friends with Winnie. In "Slipping Away" Jacqueline Woodson tells of two young women who have spent summers in a largely gay community. One young woman is now beginning to feel uncomfortable about spending summers in the company of homosexuals. "The Honorary Shepherds" by Gregory Maguire recounts the story of Lee and Pete, who are attending a private school. The two meet in film class and fall in love. Their class project is a retelling of the Nativity story with some new, honorary shepherds.

"Running," by Ellen Howard, is the story of Heather and her stepsister, Terry. Heather brings a friend home from college. Sheila is gay, and her parents have basically thrown her out of their house. Sheila stays for the summer and helps Terry see that she needs to stop running away from who she is. James Cross Giblin gives readers "Three Mondays in July," the story of David, a young man who meets Allen on the beach one

Monday. David is at first embarrassed about being caught in a rather "peeping Tom" situation, but for some reason he is drawn to the older man. Allen assures David that he is not alone and that there is no reason for David to feel ashamed of his attraction to Allen. In "Parent's Night" by Nancy Garden, Karen and her girlfriend Roxy are members of the Gay Lesbian Straight Club at their school, and the girls decide to come out to their parents in hopes of gaining acceptance. "Michael's Little Sister" by C. S. Adler ends with Becky learning that it is okay to be different. Leslea Newman's "Supper" has Meryl remembering an incredible kiss from her girlfriend. In "Holding," by Lois Lowry, Willie is off to console his father whose life partner has died. For years, Willie has allowed people to think that Chris was his father's second wife, but now Willie confronts the truth.

In "Blood Sister," which is part poem, part myth, part story, and part history, Jane Yolen tells of the relationship shared by Selna and Marda, who are blood sisters. Jonathan London's story "Hands" opens with Lon traveling by bus. He is joined by Ray, a former teacher who was accused of inappropriate behavior with one of his students. Ray has spent time in jail, but his experiences have served to make him stronger. When Ray dies of AIDS, Lon writes and recites a poem in his honor. In "50% Chance of Lightning" by Christina Salat, Robin wonders what she wants to be when she grows up. A chance walk in a storm just might hold the answer. Bay and his group live "In the Tunnels," a William Sleator story that takes place in Vietnam. The final story in the collection is "Dancing Backwards" by Marion Dane Bauer. A childhood mistake reminds Thea that it is all right to be dif-ferent even if it means that she and her girlfriend Cynthia will be thrown out of school.

Articles

Broz, William J. "Defending *Am I Blue?*" *Journal of Adolescent and Adult Literacy* 45, no. 5 (February 2002): 340–50.

Walker, K., and M. D. Bauer. "The Gay/Lesbian Connection: Two Authors Talk about Their Work." *Bookbird* 32 (summer 1994): 25–30.

Award

Kerlan Award, presented to Marion Dane Bauer by the Kerlan Friends and the Children's Literature Research Collection of the University of Minnesota Library, 1996

Challenge

Challenged at the Fairfield (Iowa) Middle School and high school libraries in 2000 because of the book's graphic description of a sexual act.

Internet

An interview with Marion Dane Bauer
   http://www.teenreads.com/authors/
   au-bauer-marion.asp

Reviews

Booklist 90 (May 15, 1994): 3915.

Bulletin of the Center for Children's Books 46 (April 1994): 251.

Horn Book 70 (July 1994): 457.

School Library Journal 40 (June 1994): 144.

Annie on My Mind

New York: Farrar, Straus and Giroux, 1982

During her freshman year as an architecture student at MIT, Liza Winthrop thinks about her joyful and painful relationship with Annie Kenyon the previous year. The two girls first meet in the Metropolitan Museum of Art when they are high school seniors. They are immediately attracted to one another and become good friends. Liza attends Foster Academy, a private school in Brooklyn, where she's student council president; Annie is a talented singer and attends a large public school. The girls visit museums, ride the Staten Island Ferry, visit each other's homes, talk on the phone, and take walks. One day Annie even smuggles Liza into her school at lunchtime. Clearly, their behavior is that of best friends. Gradually, they begin to behave as young people falling in love. They hold hands briefly, and Liza thinks about Annie, how sweet and pretty she is. Inevitably, one day they kiss. Annie has often wondered if she's gay; Liza tells Annie that she loves her. During the winter the girls continue to see each other and their affection for one another escalates.

In the meantime, events become complicated at Liza's school. One of the girls, Sally Jarrell, sets up a booth to pierce ears. After a board member's daughter is injured, Mrs. Poindexter, the headmistress, blames Liza for not informing her of the ear-piercing venture. Shortly afterward, Mrs. Poindexter suspends Liza from school. At the same time the school is having financial problems and has launched a fund-raising campaign.

When two of Liza's teachers, Ms. Stevenson and Ms. Widmer, go on spring vacation, Liza offers to feed their cats for them. This opens up an opportunity for Liza and Annie to be alone together. In an upstairs bedroom they discover a shelf of books about lesbianism, and they come to the conclusion that the two teachers are lesbians. An hour and a half before the teachers are due back from their trip, Ms. Baxter, the school secretary, appears at the door to discover the girls there by themselves. The teachers arrive, and the accusations begin. As a result of the incident and its implications, the Board of Trustees fires both teachers. Mrs. Poindexter attempts to expel Liza, but the board decides Liza should remain president of the Student Council and finds no cause for action of any kind against her. Ironically, the board directs Mrs. Poindexter and Ms. Baxter to leave at the end of the year.

When Liza and Annie visit the two teachers, Ms. Widmer tries to reassure them with these words: "Don't punish yourselves for people's ignorant reactions to what we all are." Ms. Stevenson adds, "Don't let ignorance win. Let love."

While uncertain about their relationship, Liza and Annie leave for separate universities. Interrupting this traditional narrative are letters that Liza writes to Annie revealing her thoughts about their relationship. These are letters that Liza doesn't mail, but she finally calls Annie at her dorm at Berkeley and finds out that Annie will be home for Christmas. They both cry and tell each other "I love you."

Articles

Alvine, Lynn. "Annie on My Mind." In *Rationales for Teaching Young Adult Literature,* ed. Lovann Reid and Jamie Hayes Neufield. Portland, Maine: Calendar Islands, 1999, pp. 81–88.

"Annie Goes Back to School." *School Library Journal* 42 (January 1996): 13.

Cart, Michael. "Carte Blanche: Winning One for the First Amendment." *Booklist* 92 (April 15, 1996): 1431.

Garden, Nancy. "Annie on Trial: How It Feels to Be the Author of a Challenged Book." *Voice of Youth Advocates* 19 (June 1996): 79–82.

———. "Banned: Lesbian and Gay Kids' Books under Fire." *Lambda Book Report* 4 (November/December 1994): 11–13.

———. "A Writer's Perspective on Censorship." *CSLA Journal* 23 (spring 2000): 17–18.

Gerhardt, Lillian. "Access Points." *School Library Journal* 42 (January 1996): 6.

Hoffmann, Frank. "An Interview with Nancy Garden." *Teacher Librarian* 29, no. 2 (December 2001): 59–61.

"Nancy Garden." *School Library Journal* 47 (January 2001): 17.

Awards and Prizes

Best Books for Young Adults, 1982

Best of the Best Books for Young Adults, 1970–1983

Here We Go Again: 25 Years of Best Books: Selections from 1967 to 1992

Nothin' But the Best: Best of the Best Books for Young Adults, 1966–1986

100 All-Star Choices for Teens, 2000

"Reviewer's Choice, 1982," *Booklist* 79 (Jan. 15, 1983): 671.

Challenges

U.S. District Court Judge Thomas Van Bebber ruled in 1995 that the Olathe (Kans.) School District violated the First Amendment when it removed the book from library shelves; the judge called the action "viewpoint discrimination," and he said that the removal violated Olathe students' and teachers' right to free access to information. In his order Van Bebber wrote, "Although local school boards have broad discretion in the management of school affairs, they must act within fundamental constitutional limits."

Removed in 1994 from the Chanute (Kans.) High School library shelves and access limited to those with written parental permission because of concerns about the content.

Challenged, but retained at the Liberty (Mo.) High School library in 1994.

Challenged at several Kansas City area schools in 1993 after books were donated by a national group that seeks to give young adults "fair, accurate, and inclusive images of lesbians and gay men." At the Shawnee Mission School District the book was returned to general circulation; at the Olathe East High School the book was removed; protesters burned copies of the book, but the Kansas City (Mo.) School District kept Garden's novel on the high school shelves; in Kansas City (Kans.) the school district donated the book to the city's public library; and in Lee's Summit, (Mo.), the superintendent removed the book.

Challenged, but retained at the Lapper (Mich.) West High School Library in 1993.

Challenged because it "encourages and condones" homosexuality, but retained at the Bend (Ore.) High School in 1993.

Challenged at the Cedar Mill Community Library in Portland (Ore.) in 1992 because the book portrays lesbian love and sex as normal.

Challenged in the Colony (Tex.) Public Library in 1992 because "it promotes and encourages the gay lifestyle."

Internet

Cynthia Leitich Smith, Children's Literature Resources: Interview with Children's and Young Adult Book Authors: Nancy Garden
http://www.cynthialeitichsmith.com/auth-illNancyGarden.htm

Reviews

Book Report 11 (March 1993): 65.

Booklist 78 (August 1982): 1517.

Booklist 87 (Sept. 1, 1990): 39.

Booklist 91 (Oct. 15, 1994): 413.

Booklist 95 (June 1, 1999): 1811.

Bulletin of the Center for Children's Books 36 (December 1982): 66.

Children's Book Review Service 11 (October 1982): 18.

Commonweal 111 (March 23, 1983): 176.

English Journal 73 (November 1984): 61.

Interracial Books for Children Bulletin 14 (January 1983): 35.

Journal of Reading 26 (February 1983): 468.

Kirkus Reviews 50 (June 1, 1982): 637.

Kliatt Young Adult Paperback Book Guide 18 (fall 1984): 8.

Kliatt Young Adult Paperback Book Guide 26 (November 1992): 4.

Ms. 3 (January 1993): 62.

Publishers Weekly 222 (Sept. 10, 1982): 75.

Publishers Weekly 239 (Sept. 14, 1992): 127.

School Librarian 37 (August 1989): 114.

School Library Journal 28 (August 1982): 125.

School Library Journal 41 (February 1995): 33.

School Library Journal 46 (January 2000): 54.

Voice of Youth Advocates 5 (August 1982): 30.

Voice of Youth Advocates 15 (December 1992): 320.

Athletic Shorts: Six Short Stories

New York: Greenwillow, 1991

In six short stories Crutcher's characters face real challenges. Each story is prefaced by comments from the author, and five of the six stories feature characters from four of his novels: *Chinese Handcuffs, Crazy Horse Electric Game, Running Loose,* and *Stotan.*

"A Brief Moment in the Life of Angus Bethune" spotlights Angus Bethune, a high school senior whose parents are divorced. It isn't easy being Angus. Besides being a large young man, his parents live with same-sex partners. Angus wants to be normal and socially acceptable, which is not easy given his physical size and his parents' sexual preferences. As king of the Senior Winter Ball, his greatest desire is to dance with Melissa Lefevre, senior winter ball queen, without embarrassing himself in front of his classmates. Melissa's date does his best to humiliate Angus, but Melissa is kind and tells Angus to shadow her as they dance. The technique works, and she asks Angus to escort her home. (This short story became the basis for the motion picture *Angus* in 1995.)

In "The Pin" a father and son challenge each other on a wrestling mat at a school contest. Johnny Rivers, a high school senior, loves two things in life: wrestling and puns. Johnny's dad is unreasonably strict and Johnny delights in goading him with awful puns. His dad, a former number-two wrestler at the

University of Oklahoma, requires Johnny to do ten push-ups per word. At a prelim to a parent-student volleyball game, Johnny and his dad enter into a wrestling match. They struggle back and forth until Johnny finally wears his dad down and wins. Afterwards, his dad cries and tells Johnny he wanted to treat his son better than his own father treated him.

In "The Other Pin," Petey Shropshire, a grappler in the under-125 pounds category, does not want to wrestle Chris Byers, a girl whose name is featured frequently in the local sports page. Wrestling a girl will be humiliating whether he wins or not. Then he and his friend, Johnny, see Chris and her sister at the mall, and Petey notices how pretty she is. Now he's even more reluctant to wrestle her. Something has to be done, and Petey goes to Chris's house to talk to her. He's surprised to find out that he really likes her. They devise a plan that will protect them both. On the night of the match Chris dresses as Daisy Mae and Petey dresses as Abner. They ham it up on the gym floor to the delight of the crowd and the dismay of the coaches. The two choreograph falls and pins and finally manage a mutual head butt that results in a double pin. As punishment for losing the match for his school, Petey has to run bleachers every day after practice, but it's worth it. Even if he can barely walk after running bleachers, he's going to Chris's home to take her to a movie.

In "Goin' Fishing," after Lionel Serbousek loses his parents and five-year-old brother in a boating accident, he is consumed with rage toward Neal, the friend who caused the tragedy. One summer afternoon on the lake, as Neal and his buddies were drinking beer, their boat cut Lionel's family boat in half, drowning his parents and brother. With the help of friends and Lionel's passion for swimming and art, he manages to survive. Then one day Neal comes to see him. Neal is a wreck, but Lionel won't let him come into his apartment. Then Neal's mother calls Lionel and tells him that Neal needs his forgiveness, that he's slowly dying. Lionel's friend Elaine bawls Lionel out for being so heartless and reminds him that he was drunk once before and was lucky he didn't kill anyone. Lionel yells at her that if he ever gives up his anger, he'll die, too. Later, Lionel hunts for Neal under a bridge where druggies and the homeless live. He finds Neal, makes him get his stuff, and tells him they're going fishing the next day.

Telephone Man, the main character in the story of the same name, is a high school student and a racist. He was taught by his dad that skin color matters. Telephone Man has learned to put others down to feel better about himself. Then Hawk, an African-American student, saves Telephone Man from a gang of Chinese youths, and Telephone Man becomes confused. After that incident, Telephone Man wonders if his dad is right about any of his opinions of people with skin color other than white.

In "In the Time I Get," Louie Banks meets Darren in the Buckhorn Bar during the summer after high school graduation. Darren's Uncle Gene, known as Dakota to Louie, is letting Darren stay with him because Darren is sick. Louie is working in the bar for the summer and he and Darren get to be friends. Then he learns that Darren has AIDS, and Louie is afraid his friend Carter will find out. When Darren is hospitalized and going to die, Louie visits him. Carter criticizes Louie for being a friend to a homosexual with AIDS. Louie decides that he has passed beyond Carter on that day. Louie vows, "I'm going to see how far I can go in the time I get."

Articles

Brown, J. M. "*PW* Talks with Chris Crutcher." *Publishers Weekly* 248 (March 12, 2001): 92.

Carter, Betty. "Eyes Wide Open." *School Library Journal* 45 (June 2000): 42–45.

Crutcher, Chris. "The 2000 Margaret A. Edwards Award Acceptance Speech." *Journal of Youth Services in Libraries* 13 (summer 2000): 17–19.

Davis, Terry. "A Healing Vision." *English Journal* 85 (March 1996): 36–41.

Frederick, Heather Vogel. "Chris Crutcher: 'What's Known Can't Be Unknown.'" *Publishers Weekly* 242 (Feb. 20, 1995): 183–84.

Halls, Kelly Milner. "Story Behind the Story: Crutcher's People." *Booklist* 97 (April 1, 2001): 1463.

Jenkinson, Dave. "Portraits: Chris Crutcher." *Emergency Librarian* 18 (January/February 1991): 67–71.

Lesesne, Teri S. "Banned in Berlin: An Interview with Chris Crutcher." *Emergency Librarian* 23 (May/June 1996): 61–63.

McDonnell, Christine. "New Voices, New Visions: Chris Crutcher." *Horn Book* 64 (May 1988): 332.

Raymond, A. "Chris Crutcher: Helps Teachers Know Kids." *Teaching PreK–8* 20 (February 1990): 42–44.

Weaver, Matthew. "Chris Crutcher's Balancing Act: Cool Old Guy Meets Brash Young Writer." *Voice of Youth Advocates* 24 (August 2001): 182–85.

Awards and Prizes

Best Books for Young Adults, 1992

Here We Go Again: 25 Years of Best Books: Selections from 1967 to 1992

Margaret A. Edwards Award, 2000

100 All-Star Choices for Teens, 2000

Books

Davis, T. *Presenting Chris Crutcher.* New York: Twayne/Prentice-Hall, 1997.

Speaking for Ourselves: Autobiographical Sketches by Notable Authors of Books for Young Adults. Edited by D. R. Gallo. Urbana, Ill.: National Council of Teachers of English, 1990, p. 59.

Challenges

Pulled from the elementary school collections, but retained at the middle school libraries in Anchorage (Alaska) in 1999. A parent challenged the book because of its lack of respect for parents and God, its treatment of homosexuality, and its bad language.

Challenged at the Charleston County (S.C.) School Library in 1995 because the book deals with divorce, violence, AIDS, and homosexuality.

Internet

Booksense.com, Very Interesting People: Chris Crutcher
http://www.booksense.com/people/archive/crutcherchris.jsp

Chris Crutcher, Official Author Web Site
http://www.aboutcrutcher.com

Learning about Chris Crutcher
http://www.scils.rutgers.edu/~kvander/crutcher.html

Teachers@Random, Authors/Illustrators: Chris Crutcher
http://randomhouse.com/teachers/authors/crut.html

Reviews

ALAN Review 19 (fall 1991): 34.

Book Report 10 (January 1992): 50.

Booklist 88 (Oct. 15, 1991): 428.

Bulletin of the Center for Children's Books 45 (December 1991): 87.

English Journal 81 (April 1992): 85+.

Horn Book 67 (September/October 1991): 602.

Journal of Reading 35 (May 1992): 684+.

Publishers Weekly 238 (Aug. 23, 1991): 63.

School Library Journal 37 (September 1991): 278.

Voice of Youth Advocates 15 (April 1992): 26.

Video

Angus, available on VHS from Turner Home Entertainment. 1995. Dawn Steel and Charles Loven. 87 minutes.

Baby Be-Bop

New York: HarperCollins, 1995

Block combines elements of realism and fantasy in her books about Weetzie Bat and her friends and family, which include *Weetzie Bat, Cherokee Bat and the Goat Guys, Witch Baby,* and *Missing Angel Juan*. This combination results in a genre known as "magical realism." The narrative of *Baby Be-Bop* is divided into two parts.

Part One

Dirk's parents were killed in a car crash when he was quite young, and Dirk was sent to live with his grandmother after the accident. Dirk has known he is gay since his childhood. His Grandma Fifi, though, thinks this is merely a phase which Dirk will grow out of one day soon. Dirk keeps his sexuality a secret from his friends and classmates until he meets Pup Lambert. The two become immediate friends. Pup appears to be surviving on his own, though he lives with his mother and her succession of boyfriends. Dirk loves Pup but cannot seem to bring himself to reveal his true feelings for fear of being rejected. One day, after Dirk and Pup have gone surfing, they hitchhike a ride home. The two are picked up by two girls from their school. Pup and Dirk return home with the girls, and Dirk is surprised when Pup kisses Tracey. Though he tries to follow suit by kissing Nancy, Dirk knows in his heart he would rather be kissing Pup. When Dirk finally does confess his true feelings to Pup, Pup leaves. Dirk becomes a loner.

For his sixteenth birthday, Grandma Fifi gives Dirk her beautiful 1955 convertible. The car's hood ornament is a lamp, vaguely reminiscent of Aladdin's magic lamp. Fifi tells Dirk he can share his secrets with the lamp. Dirk, however, thinks he has no story to tell. He feels dead inside now that Pup is gone from his life. Instead, Dirk visits punk night clubs where he slam dances himself into oblivion. One night he is confronted by a pack of skinheads who attack Dirk and leave him for dead in the parking lot.

Part Two

Dirk manages to drive home after the attack. He removes the lamp hood ornament from the car and takes it into his room, requesting that it tell him a story to help ease his pain. Suddenly, a young woman appears in Dirk's bedroom. Dirk asks her for her story; Gazelle replies by telling Dirk that she, too, is an orphan like him. She lived with her aunt after the death of her parents, an aunt who treated her rather cruelly. Gazelle's aunt was a seamstress, and Gazelle helped her with the sewing. One day a stranger appeared at her aunt's door and asked Gazelle to make a dress for his beloved. When he returned for the dress, he asked Gazelle to

9

model the dress for him. In return, he gave her the dress and a lamp. Gazelle learned later that she was pregnant. Her aunt died, and Gazelle gave birth to a baby girl who would become Dirk's Grandma Fifi. Before Gazelle disappears, she tells Dirk that "any love that is love is right."

The next person to appear in Dirk's room is his deceased father, Dirby McDonald, Fifi's only child. Dirby relates the story of his life as a poet and his love for Dirk's mother, Just Silver. Even though his life is over, Dirby tells Dirk to go on. Dirk tells his story to the lamp. When he is finished, a genie emerges from the lamp who takes Dirk on a trip to Duck's House. Now Duck tells his story to Dirk. The moral of all these stories is that in order to heal, one must tell one's story with honesty. Dirk awakens from his almost dreamlike state in the hospital with Fifi. He now knows that stories can hurt but will ultimately set him free.

Article

Platzner, Rebecca. "Collage in Francesca Lia Block's *Weetzie Bat* Books." *ALAN Review* 25, no. 2 (winter 1998): 23–26.

Book

Cart, Michael. *Presenting Francesca Lia Block*. Boston: Twayne Publishers, 1998.

Challenges

Removed from the mandatory reading program at the Norman L. Sullivan Middle School in Bonsall (Calif.) in 2000 due to sexually explicit language.

Removed from the Barron (Wis.) School District in 1998 because of the book's use of vulgar language and sexually explicit passages. The ACLU of Wisconsin filed suit against the school district on Feb. 16, 1999. The books were then returned to the library while a federal court considered the lawsuit. On Oct. 8, 1999, it was agreed that the novel would remain available to students as part of the school district's settlement of the federal lawsuit.

Internet

A conversation with Francesca Lia Block
  http://www.writes.org/conversations/
  conver_2.html

Reviews

Booklist 71 (Oct. 1, 1995): 308.

Bulletin of the Center for Children's Books 49 (October 1995): 46.

Horn Book 92 (March 1996): 202.

School Library Journal 41 (September 1995): 218.

The Catcher in the Rye

Boston: Little, Brown, 1951

Holden Caulfield has been kicked out of several prep schools. The latest disaster is Pencey Prep School, where sixteen-year-old Holden is flunking four courses and not applying himself. He is told not to return to the school after Christmas vacation. Holden expects his parents to be furious with him. He decides to leave the school early but doesn't want to get home before his parents have received the letter informing them of his failure. Once Holden leaves the school, his adventures during three days in New York City begin.

Before leaving Pencey he rants about a few of the people who have made his life miserable. On Saturday night his good-looking roommate, Stradlater, made a mistake dating Jane Gallagher, a childhood friend of Holden's. Ackley, his pimply, nosy neighbor, refused to let him sleep in his room after Holden and Stradlater fought. A goodbye visit to an elderly teacher of Holden's further depresses him and helps him decide to leave school early Saturday morning instead of waiting until Wednesday, when he would usually return home before the Christmas holidays.

Holden takes the train from Agerstown, Pa., the location of Pencey Prep, to New York City. He gets a room at the Edmont Hotel, a place he decides is "lousy with perverts." Because he's lonesome and horny, he thinks about girls to call. He decides to go to the hotel nightclub by himself. In the Lavender Room he joins three young women who are visiting the city, and he drinks and dances with them until they abruptly leave. He keeps thinking about his friend, Jane Gallagher, and how much he misses her. Then he takes a cab to Ernie's, a piano bar he knows in Greenwich Village. Holden doesn't stay long and ends up walking forty-one blocks back to his hotel because he is tired of riding in taxicabs. Once back in the hotel he is approached by a man in the elevator offering to send a prostitute to his room. Holden agrees to the arrangement but then tells Sunny, the prostitute, he isn't in the mood, pays her, and she leaves.

On Sunday Holden continues his encounters with a variety of people. He meets two nuns at breakfast; he buys a record for Phoebe, his little sister; and he takes Sally Hayes, a girl he has dated, to the movies and ice skating. Afterwards, he meets Carl Luce, his student advisor at another school, at a bar where Holden gets terribly drunk. He rests in Central Park and then sneaks into his own house and wakes up Phoebe. Of all the people Holden meets and talks about, Phoebe is obviously his favorite. She is appalled that he has flunked out of another school and confirms what he already knows: "Daddy is going to kill you!" Finally, Holden knows he needs to leave before his parents get home, so he calls up Mr. Antolini, a favorite teacher, and arranges to spend the night at his house. Then he thinks that Mr. Antolini is putting the moves on him, so he leaves abruptly and sleeps in Grand Central station.

Holden delivers a message to Phoebe's school for her to meet him at the art museum. He has decided to leave and go out West. When she arrives, she's dragging her suitcase and tells him she's going with him. They end up at the zoo with Phoebe riding the carousel and Holden crying.

After his expulsion from Pencey Prep and his escapades in New York City, Holden has an emotional and physical breakdown and is sent to recover in California, where his brother B.D. lives. Holden tells his story as he is recovering and expecting to be sent to a new school in September.

Articles

Barr, Donald. "Should Holden Caulfield Read These Books?" *New York Times Book Review* 91 (May 4, 1986): 50–51.

Bryan, James E. "The Psychological Structure of *The Catcher in the Rye*." *PMLA* 89 (October 1974): 1064–74.

Coles, Robert. "Reconsideration: J. D. Salinger." *New Republic* 168 (April 28, 1973): 30–32.

Costello, Donald P. "The Language of *The Catcher in the Rye*." *American Speech* 34 (October 1959): 172–81.

De Luca, Geraldine. "Unself-Conscious Voices: Larger Contexts for Adolescents." *The Lion and the Unicorn* 2 (fall 1978): 89–108.

Glasser, William. "The Catcher in the Rye." *Michigan Quarterly Review* 15 (fall 1976): 432–55.

Kaplan, Charles. "Holden and Huck: The Odyssey of Youth." *College English* 28 (November 1956): 76–80.

Kazin, Alfred. "J. D. Salinger: Everybody's Favorite." *Atlantic* 208 (August 1961): 27–31.

McCarthy, Mary. "J. D. Salinger's Closed Circuit." *Harper's Magazine* 225 (October 1962): 46–48.

Moss, A. "Catcher Comes of Age." *Esquire* 96 (December 1981): 56–58+.

Ohmann, Carol, and Richard Ohmann. "Reviews, Critics, and *The Catcher in the Rye*." *Critical Inquiry* 3 (fall 1976): 15–38.

Pinsker, S. "*The Catcher in the Rye* and All: Is the Age of Formative Books Over?" *Georgia Review* 40 (winter 1986): 953–67.

Slabey, Robert M. "*The Catcher in the Rye:* Christian Theme and Symbol." *College Language Association Journal* 6 (March 1963): 170–83.

"Special Number: Salinger." *Wisconsin Studies in Contemporary Literature* 4 (winter 1963): 1–160.

Strauch, Carl F. "King in the Back Row: Meaning through Structure—A Reading of Salinger's *The Catcher in the Rye*." *Wisconsin Studies in Contemporary Literature* 2 (winter 1961): 5–30.

Teachout, T. "Salinger Then and Now." *Commentary* 84 (September 1987): 61–64.

Books

French, Warren. *J. D. Salinger*. 2nd rev. ed. Twayne's U.S. Author Series. Boston: G. K. Hall, 1976.

Hamilton, Ian. *In Search of J. D. Salinger*. New York: Vintage Books, 1989.

J. D. Salinger. Edited by Harold Bloom. New York: Chelsea House, 1987.

Salinger: A Critical and Personal Portrait. Edited by Henry A. Grunwald. New York: Harper, 1962.

Salinger, M. *Dream Catcher.* New York: Washington Square, 2000.

With Love and Squalor. Edited by K. Kotzen and T. Beller. New York: Broadway Books, 2001.

Challenges

The book was challenged, but retained on the shelves of the Limestone County (Ala.) school district in 2000 despite objections to its foul language.

Banned, but later reinstated after community protests at the Windsor Forest High School in Savannah (Ga.) in 2000. The controversy began in early 1999 when a parent complained about sex, violence, and profanity in the book, which was part of an advanced-placement English class.

Removed because of profanity and sexual situations from the required reading curriculum of the Marysville (Calif.) Joint Unified School District in 1997. The school superintendent removed it to get it "out of the way so that we didn't have that polarization over a book."

Challenged, but retained at the Glynn Academy High School in Brunswick (Ga.) in 1997. A student had objected to the novel's profanity and sexual references.

Challenged at the Oxford Hills High School in Paris (Maine) in 1996. A parent had objected to the use of "the F word."

Challenged at the St. John's County Schools in St. Augustine (Fla.) in 1995.

Challenged as mandatory reading in the Goffstown (N.H.) schools in 1994 because of the vulgar words used and the sexual exploits experienced in the book.

Challenged, but retained at the New Richmond (Wis.) High School in 1994 for use in some English classes.

Challenged as required reading in the Corona-Norco (Calif.) Unified School District in 1993 because it is "centered around negative activity." The book was retained, and teachers could select alternatives if students objected to Salinger's novel.

Challenged at the Cumberland Valley High School in Carlisle (Pa.) in 1992 because of a parent's objections that it contains profanity and is immoral.

Challenged in Waterloo (Iowa) schools and Duval County (Fla.) public school libraries in 1992 because of profanity, lurid passages about sex, and statements defamatory to minorities, God, women, and the disabled.

Challenged at the Jamaica High School in Sidell (N.Y.) in 1992 because the book contains profanities and depicts premarital sex, alcohol abuse, and prostitution.

Challenged at the Grayslake (Ill.) Community High School in 1991.

Because the book contains profanity, it was banned from the classrooms in the Boron (Calif.) High School in 1989.

Reviews

Atlantic 188 (August 1951): 82.

Booklist 47 (July 15, 1951): 401.

Booklist 91 (June 1, 1995): 1761.

Catholic World 174 (November 1951): 154.

Chicago Tribune, July 15, 1951, p. 3.

Choice 31 (October 1993): 292.

Christian Science Monitor 43 (July 19, 1951): 7.

English Journal 81 (April 1992): 87.

English Journal 82 (April 1993): 88.

Kirkus Reviews 19 (May 15, 1951): 247.

Library Journal 76 (July 1951): 1125.

Nation 173 (Sept. 1, 1951): 3.

New Republic 125 (July 16, 1951): 20.

New York Herald Tribune Book Review, July 15, 1951, p. 3.

New York Times, July 15, 1951, p. 5.

New Yorker 27 (Aug. 11, 1951): 89.

Newsweek 38 (July 16, 1951): 89.

San Francisco Chronicle, July 15, 1951, p. 17.

Saturday Review 34 (July 14, 1951): 12.

Time 58 (July 16, 1951): 96.

Times Literary Supplement, Sept. 7, 1951, p. 561.

Voice of Youth Advocates 16 (February 1994): 410.

Videos

The Catcher in the Rye. In "Man's Search for Identity." Producer: Center for Humanities, Communications Park, Box 1000, Mt. Kisco, NY 10549-0101. Distributor: Guidance Associates, 90 South Bedford Road, Mt. Kisco, NY 10549; (800) 431-1242.

Kile, T. S., and K. Clubb. *Salinger: Redemption in Manhattan.* Waterford, Conn.: The Company, 1995. 24 minutes.

The Chocolate War

New York: Pantheon, 1974

For many teens, the first year in high school is a time of transition, a time of challenge, a time of discovery. Jerry Renault's freshman year at Trinity High School holds many challenges. His transition is made all the more difficult, however, due to the recent death of his mother. Jerry's father, still in his own throes of grief, seems distant and unable to help his son deal with the loss. Jerry throws himself into the life of his new school. He tries out for the football team despite his slender build, determined to demonstrate to the coach what another player calls "guts." There he meets and becomes friends with Goober. Goober questions the wisdom of the quote on the poster in Jerry's locker about "disturbing the universe." Perhaps it is wiser to keep a low profile, to try to fit in. At Trinity High School, fitting in means following the rules of the religious brothers who staff the classrooms.

However, there is another group of leaders who must be followed at Trinity. The group known as the Vigils determines who will and will not succeed at the school. Archie, their leader, tests each freshman to see if he can measure up to Vigil standards. Archie's tasks are not simple pranks; he sets up elaborate schemes designed to test the mettle of any young man. For Goober, the task is to loosen the various nuts and bolts which hold together the desks and chairs in Brother Eugene's classroom. The classroom furniture will then collapse with little movement.

Jerry's task will place him at odds with all of the other students in the school. Under Archie's direction, Jerry refuses to sell the chocolates for the annual school fundraiser. Each morning, as other students relate their success, Jerry must rise and continue to refuse to participate. His harshest critic is Brother Leon, whose very job rests with a successful sale of all the chocolates. Jerry takes the emotional abuse leveled at him by Leon, and he even endures a physical pummeling from the Neanderthal-like Emil. Still, Jerry persists. When Archie informs Jerry that his test is over and that he may now sell chocolates, Jerry refuses. This refusal sets up a final confrontation between Jerry and the Vigils, a confrontation in which Jerry and Emil will meet in a boxing match. Bowed and bloodied by the beating he receives from Emil, Jerry tells Goober that perhaps it is wrong to disturb the universe. Perhaps, in the end, one person can stand only so long against the will of others who are more powerful.

Articles

Ellis, W. G. "Cormier and the Pessimistic View." *ALAN Review* 12 (winter 1985): 10–12, 52–53.

MacLeod, A. S. "Robert Cormier and the Adolescent Novel." *Children's Literature in Education* 12 (summer 1981): 74–81.

March-Penny, R. "From Hardback to Paperback: *The Chocolate War,* by Robert Cormier." *Children's Literature in Education* 9 (summer 1978): 78–84.

Nodelman, P. "Robert Cormier Does a Number." *Children's Literature in Education* 14 (summer 1983): 94–103.

Silvey, A. "An Interview with Robert Cormier." *Horn Book* 61 (March/April 1985): 145–55.

_____. "An Interview with Robert Cormier." *Horn Book* 61 (May/June 1985): 289–96.

West, M. I. "Censorship on Children's Books: Authors and Editors Provide New Perspectives on the Issue." *Publishers Weekly* 218 (July 1987): 108–11.

Awards and Prizes

ALAN Award, 1983

Best of the Best Books for Young Adults, 1970–1983

Lewis Carroll Shelf Award, 1979

Margaret A. Edwards Award, 1991

Nothin' But the Best: Best of the Best Books for Young Adults, 1966–1986

100 All-Star Choices for Teens, 2000

Still Alive: The Best of the Best Books for Young Adults, 1960–1974

Books

Campbell, Patty. *Presenting Robert Cormier.* New York: Dell, 1989.

Challenges

The Chocolate War was challenged at a local board of education meeting in Lisbon (Ohio) in 2001 as a "pornographic" book that should be removed from high school English classes.

Retained as optional reading for eighth-graders at Rice Avenue Middle School in Girard (Pa.) in 2000. A grandmother found the book offensive and did not want her granddaughters reading it.

Challenged on the eighth-grade reading list of the Lancaster (Mass.) school district in 2000 due to the book's content and language.

Challenged as part of the Silverheels Middle School's supplemental reading material in South Park (Colo.) in 2000 because parents objected to sexually suggestive language in the book.

Challenged at the Maple Heights (Ohio) School in 2000 because "the book teaches immorality."

Challenged on the York County (Va.) schools' reading list and in classrooms in 1999 and 2000 because the book contains profanity and violence.

Challenged on the required reading list for ninth-graders at Colton (N.Y.) schools in 1999 due to its references to masturbation, profanity, disrespect for women, and sexual innuendo.

Banned from the Broken Arrow (Okla.) schools in 1998 because it is the "antithesis of the district's character development curriculum." The board of education is considering forming a parent committee to review all books listed on the district's electronic bookshelf and to design a ratings system for more than 400 titles found there.

Removed from the Greenville (Tex.) Intermediate School library in 1998 because "it contained blasphemy, profanity, and graphic sexual passages."

Challenged in the Stroudsburg (Pa.) ninth-grade curriculum in 1996 after complaints about the novel's language and content.

Removed from middle school libraries in the Riverside (Calif.) Unified School District in 1996 as inappropriate for seventh- and eighth-graders to read without class discussion due to its mature themes, sexual situations, and smoking.

Challenged at the Nauset Regional Middle School in Orleans (Mass.) in 1995 due to profanity and sexually explicit language.

Removed from the Grosse Pointe (Mich.) School District library shelves in 1995 because it deals with "gangs, peer pressure, and learning to make your own decisions."

Returned to the Hephzibah High School tenth-grade reading list in Augusta (Ga.) in 1994 after the complainant said, "I don't see anything educational about that book. If they ever send a book like that home with one of my daughters again I will personally burn it and throw the ashes on the principal's desk."

Challenged as required reading in the Hudson Falls (N.Y.) schools in 1994 because the book has recurring themes of rape, masturbation, violence, and degrading treatment of women.

Challenged in the Kyrene (Ariz.) elementary schools in 1993 because of a masturbation scene.

Challenged at the New Milford (Conn.) schools in 1992 because the novel contains language, sexual references, violence, subjectivity, and negativism that are harmful to students.

Suspended from classroom use, pending review, at the Woodsville High School in Haverhill (N.H.) in 1990 because the novel contains expletives, references to masturbation and sexual fantasies, and

derogatory characterizations of a teacher and of religious ceremonies.

Challenged as suitable curriculum material in the Harwinton and Burlington (Conn.) schools in 1990 because it contains profanity and subject matter that set bad examples and give students negative views of life.

The West Hernando (Fla.) Middle School principal recommended in 1988 that Cormier's novel be removed from the school library shelves because it is "inappropriate."

Challenged at the Moreno Valley (Calif.) Unified School District libraries in 1987 because it "contains profanity, sexual situations, and themes that allegedly encourage disrespectful behavior."

Removed from the Panama City (Fla.) school classrooms and libraries in 1986 because of "offensive" language.

Challenged at Barnstable High School in Hyannis (Mass.) in 1986 because of the novel's profanity, "obscene references to masturbation and sexual fantasies," and "ultimately because of its pessimistic ending." The novel, complainants said, fostered negative impressions of authority, of school systems, and of religious schools.

Challenged at the Cornwall (N.Y.) High School in 1985 because the novel is "humanistic and destructive of religious and moral beliefs and of national spirit."

Banned from the Stroudsburg (Pa.) High School library in 1985 because it is "blatantly graphic, pornographic and wholly unacceptable for a high school library."

Banned from the Richmond Two School District's middle school libraries in Columbia (S.C.) in 1984 due to "language problems," but later reinstated for eighth-graders only.

Removed from the Lake Havasu (Ariz.) High School freshman reading list in

1984. The school district board charged the Havasu teachers with failing to set good examples for students, fostering disrespect in the classroom, and failing to support the board.

Challenged at the Richmond (R.I.) High School in 1983 because the book was deemed "pornographic" and "repulsive."

Removed from the Liberty High School in Westminster (Md.) in 1982 due to the book's "foul language," portrayal of violence, and degradation of schools and teachers.

Challenged and temporarily removed from the English curriculum in two Lapeer (Mich.) high schools in 1981 because of "offensive language and explicit descriptions of sexual situations in the book."

Internet

"The Chocolate War" Teaching Guide
http://www.mcdougallittell.com/lit/litcon/chocolat/guide.htm

"Duel at High Noon: A Replay of Cormier's Works": Online article from the ALAN Review
http://scholar.lib.vt.edu/ejournals/ALAN/winter94/Headley.html

Internet Public Library: Information about Cormier and his writing
http://www.ipl.org/youth/AskAuthor/Cormier.html

"The People vs. Robert Cormier": ACLU news story about Cormier and book challenges
http://www.aclu.org/news/w011097a.html

Other Resources

The Chocolate War. Motion picture. MCEG/Sterling Distributors, 1988. 100 minutes. Rated R.

A Talk with Robert Cormier. Video interview. Tim Podell Productions. 18 minutes.

Reviews

American Libraries 130 (October 1974): 492.

Booklist 71 (March 15, 1975): 747.

English Journal 62 (January 1975): 112.

Horn Book 55 (April 1979): 217.

Kirkus Reviews 42 (April 1974): 371.

Library Journal 99 (May 1974): 1450.

New York Times Book Review, May 5, 1974, p. 15.

Publishers Weekly 205 (April 15, 1974): 52.

School Library Journal 29 (November 1982): 35.

A Day No Pigs Would Die

New York: Alfred Knopf, 1972

The novel begins with twelve-year-old Robert saving a Holstein cow's life. The cow has several problems when Robert hears her bawling. She has twin calves that need help being born, and she's choking on a huge goiter in her throat. At great physical risk Robert births the calves messily and dramatically and yanks out the goiter. It takes him a week to recuperate from his wounds sufficiently to return to school.

Robert lives with his parents and his Aunt Carrie on a Shaker farm in Learning, Vt. His father, Haven, kills pigs to make enough money to keep the farm, and the stench of killing is always on him. After Robert saves the neighbor's cow and her calves, the neighbor gives him a newborn white pig that Robert names Pinky. Since his family is poor, Robert has owned little of his own and is thrilled to have a pig as a pet. He spends many happy hours playing with Pinky and watching her grow into a 300-pound sow.

During his twelfth year Robert has some adventures that help him learn about the world. His father takes him on a trip to the cemetery late at night where they witness a man removing a baby's coffin from a grave. Apparently, the man had been having an affair and the dead baby was his child.

The highlight of Robert's year is his trip with the Tanners to Rutland Fair where he shows the matched yearlings, Bib and Bob, and where Pinky wins first prize for best-behaved pig. Other events are traumatic for Robert, though. He witnesses a dog being weaseled, and the dog is so badly hurt that its owner has to kill it. Then he and his father think that Pinky is barren but arrange to have her bred to Samson, a 600-pound pig who mounts Pinky and obviously hurts her. Finally, Robert experiences the death of loved ones. He endures the slaughter of his pet pig, because the family needs the meat to survive the winter. And worst of all, his father dies and leaves Robert in charge of the farm at the tender age of thirteen.

Throughout these events—the gift, the desecration of the grave, the hints of adultery, the deaths of Pinky and his father—there is an understated humor in the voice of a boy on the brink of manhood. Robert doesn't quite understand everything he hears and sees, but he's learning. He has to learn fast to be able to shoulder the responsibility his father has left with him. The farm, his mother, and his aunt are now dependent upon him.

Articles

Peck, Robert Newton. "Dear Rob: How to Write to an Author, Get Him to Write Back, or Be Ignored." *Book Report* 18 (September/October 1999): 33–34.

———. "How to Torture an Author." *Library Talk* 10 (November/December 1997): 34.

———. "Intellectual Rob." *Book Report* 11 (March/April 1993): 67+.

Awards and Prizes

Best Books for Young Adults, 1973

Colorado Children's Book Award, 1977

Media and Methods Maxi Award for Best Paperback, 1975

Still Alive: The Best of the Best Books for Young Adults, 1960–1974

Books

Peck, Robert Newton. *Fiction Is Folks: How to Create Unforgettable Characters*. Cincinnati, Ohio: Writer's Digest, 1983.

———. *Secrets of Successful Fiction*. Cincinnati, Ohio: Writer's Digest, 1980.

Challenges

Banned from the St. Lawrence School in Utica (Mich.) in 1997 because of a passage involving pig breeding. The teacher quit her job over the banning of the novel.

Challenged at the Anderson (Mo.) Junior High School in 1996 because of its content.

Pulled from an Anderson (S.C.) middle school library in 1995 because of the "gory" descriptions of two pigs mating, a pig being slaughtered, and a cow giving birth.

Challenged at the Pawhuska (Okla.) middle school in 1995 because the book uses bad language, gives "gory" details of mating, and lacks religious values.

Removed from seventh-grade classes at the Payson (Utah) Middle School in 1994 after several parents "had problems with language, with animal breeding, and with a scene that involves an infant grave exhumation."

Challenged but retained on the shelves of the Waupaca (Wis.) school libraries in 1994 after a parent "objected to graphic passages dealing with sexuality in the book."

Challenged at the Sherwood Elementary School in Melbourne (Fla.) in 1993 because the book could give the "impression that rape and violence are acceptable." The comment was made in reference to a descriptive passage about a boar mating with a sow in the barnyard.

Challenged as suitable curriculum material in the Harwinton and Burlington (Conn.) schools in 1990 because it contains language and subject matter that set bad examples and give students negative views of life.

Challenged in Jefferson County (Colo.) school libraries in 1988 because "it is bigoted against Baptists and women and depicts violence, hatred, animal cruelty, and murder."

Internet

Educational Paperback Association: Robert Newton Peck

http://www.edupaperback.org/pastbios/Peckrob.html

Good Conversations! Robert Newton Peck

http://www.goodconversations.com/authors/peck.html

Robert Newton Peck, Official Author Web Site

http://my.athenet.net/~blahnik/rnpeck/

Reviews

Atlantic 231 (April 1973): 114.

Booklist 82 (March 1, 1986): 975.

Booklist 87 (Feb. 15, 1991): 1185.

Booklist 88 (Feb. 15, 1992): 1101.

Booklist 90 (June 1, 1994): 1799.

Bulletin of the Center for Children's Books 26 (May 1973): 142.

Christian Science Monitor, Jan. 17, 1973, p. 11.

Emergency Librarian 9 (January 1982): 17.

English Journal 69 (September 1980): 87.

Horn Book 49 (October 1973): 472.

Kirkus Reviews 40 (Oct. 15, 1972): 1215.

Kirkus Reviews 40 (Nov. 1, 1972): 1258.

Library Journal 97 (Nov. 15, 1972): 3728.

Library Journal 98 (March 15, 1973): 1022.

New York Times, Jan. 4, 1973, p. 35.

New York Times Book Review, May 13, 1973, p. 37.

New Yorker 48 (Feb. 3, 1973): 100.

Newsweek 81 (March 12, 1973): 96.

Publishers Weekly 202 (Oct. 30, 1972): 49.

Publishers Weekly 204 (Oct. 22, 1973): 112.

Saturday Review 1 (Jan. 13, 1973): 66.

School Library Journal 29 (August 1983): 27.

Times Literary Supplement, Aug. 17, 1973, p. 945.

Wilson Library Bulletin 49 (March 1975): 517.

Video

A Talk with Robert Newton Peck. Tom Podell Productions, 1998. 20 minutes. Tom Podell Productions, P.O. Box 244, Scarborough, NY 10510; phone: (800) 642-4181; http://www.goodconversations.com.

BETTE GREENE

The Drowning of Stephan Jones

New York: Delacorte, 1991

Carla is a girl on a mission. She will somehow make Andy Harris notice her. Resolutely, she marches down to Harris's hardware store, determined to make a big impression. A chance encounter with two strangers in the hardware store will change her life in ways she cannot even begin to imagine. Rachetville, Ark., has a deservedly tough reputation. This town is no place for anyone "different." That applies not only to Carla's mother, the town's outspoken librarian, but also to the two newcomers Carla meets at Harris's store. Frank and Stephan are accosted by one of the women in the store who overhears Frank calling Stephan his "love." Frank stands up to the woman and to the Harris men. Stephan seems ready to bolt and run given the chance.

Carla cannot move or speak. It is bad enough her mother has managed to make enemies in town; Carla would just like to get along and be relatively unnoticed. When Andy stops her at school, Carla is dismayed when the conversation quickly turns to Frank and Stephan. It is immediately clear that Andy is prejudiced about homosexuality. Carla is upset by Andy's reaction, but her attraction to him prevents her from defending Frank and Stephan. In fact, Carla manages to convince her mother to attend the Christmas services at Andy's church. There, though the preacher delivers a sermon condemning homosexuality, Carla seems not to hear the words. Later that day, Andy shows up at Carla's house with an unexpected Christmas gift. Soon, the two are an inseparable couple.

Frank and Stephan have opened a small antique shop in a town near Rachetville. One day, Andy and two of his friends, Spider and Ironman, encounter Stephan in his local pizza parlor. They follow him from there and chase him into an alley, where they bully Stephan, burning his face with the steaming pizza. This is not the end of the harassment, as Andy begins a campaign to bully the two men into leaving their store and the community. He makes crank phone calls to Frank and Stephan. Though Carla is aware of these activities, she goes along with Andy and his friends, who see the calls as just simple pranks. Threatening letters soon are added to Andy's campaign of bullying. Again, Carla decides to do nothing to stop the torment. Her mind is more preoccupied with plans for the upcoming dance.

Frank and Stephan want to end the threats being made by Andy Harris. Determining that going to the police is not a viable option, they decide instead to contact Reverend Wheelright, the pastor of Andy's church. Wheelright offers no assistance to the two, however, and Andy's harassment continues. On the night of the prom, the paths of Andy and Carla and Frank and Stephan intersect.

Andy and his friends chase Stephan, ultimately hurling him into a river where he drowns. Andy stands trial for the murder of Stephan Jones; Carla is the key witness against him. Andy claims his act was caused by Stephan's advances. He and the others involved are given suspended sentences and probation. In the midst of Andy's celebration, Frank appears. He confronts Andy and shows all those gathered there the "love letters" Andy wrote to Stephan. Andy is discredited in the eyes of all those he knows. Carla and her mother leave Rachetville.

Articles

Finnessy, Patrick K. "Drowning in Dichotomy: Interpreting *The Drowning of Stephan Jones*." *ALAN Review* 25, no. 3 (spring 1998): 24–27.

Greene, Bette. "America's Designated Victims: Our Creative Young." *ALAN Review* 20, no. 2 (winter 1994): 2–5.

Challenges

The book was removed from the Barron (Wis.) School District in 1998. The ACLU sued the district and the book will remain available to students.

Banned from the Mascenic Regional High School in Ipswich (N.H.) in 1995.

Removed from the curriculum and school library shelves in Boling (Tex.) in 1993.

Internet

Frequently asked questions about the novel, from Bette Greene's home page

http://www.bettegreene.com/stephanfaqs.htm

Online article from the ALAN Review (winter 1994)

http://scholar.lib.vt.edu/ejournals/ALAN/winter94/Greene.html

Online article from the ALAN Review (spring 1998)

http://scholar.lib.vt.edu/ejournals/ALAN/spring98/finnessy.html

Reviews

Booklist 88 (Feb. 1, 1992): 1018.

Kirkus Reviews 59 (Nov. 15, 1991): 1470.

School Library Journal 37 (October 1991): 142.

Voice of Youth Advocates 14 (December 1991): 312.

Fallen Angels

New York: Scholastic, 1988

After high school graduation, many young men begin to plan their college careers or select their vocation. Perry is at loose ends as his senior year comes to an end and so he decides to enlist in the Army. He is sent from New York to basic training, after which he is shipped to Vietnam. The war, according to all the press reports, is not expected to last much longer. However, Perry soon discovers that the war is still very much a reality for the members of Alpha Company. At first, Perry and his fellow soldiers battle little more than mosquitoes, malaria, and the damp rot of the jungle. Before too long, though, Perry is in the thick of the fighting. Alongside Perry are the other members of Alpha Company. Monaco is of Italian descent, and Gates is from Chicago. Peewee is the jokester of the group, always ready to crack wise. Lobel sees every situation as if it were part of a movie. Jenkins and Johnson round out the group.

Alpha Company is part of the 196th Division stationed at Chu Lai. Their task is to fight the Vietcong, also known as "Charlie." Some of the fighting is out in the open, but much of it involves avoiding land mines and other traps set by the enemy in the jungle and rice paddies. Perry and his company must also visit villages, seeking anyone who might be friendly to Charlie. As the war intensifies, Perry and his company are often sent out to assist other units in the field. The chopper rides are terrifying to Perry. Even more frightening are the body bags stacked and waiting for those who lose their lives in battle. When his fellow soldier Jenkins is killed by a mine, Perry is rattled. The senseless death of his friend is too reminiscent of the gang slayings back home in New York. Perry fears not just for his own life, but for the well-being of the men who have come to be his friends in this dangerous country.

As the war progresses, Perry comes to understand more of the politics behind the fighting. Newsmen cover some of the battles searching only for comforting sound bites to play for anxious viewers back home. Politicians keep insisting that the war is coming to an end, that the enemy is disheartened. "The war is almost over" seems to be the politicians' mantra. Perry is wounded twice before receiving his orders to return to New York and his family. However, when Perry returns stateside, he knows life will never be the same for him. He has left part of himself and his innocence in Vietnam.

Articles

Kazemek, Francis E. "Literature of Vietnam and Afghanistan: Exploring War and Peace with Adolescents." *ALAN Review* 23, no. 3 (spring 1996): 6–9.

Kutzer, M. Daphne, ed. *Writers of Multicultural Fiction for Young Adults.* Westwood, Conn.: Greenwood, 1996, pp. 299–305.

Moore, John Noell. "'Motherly Business' and the Moves to Manhood." *ALAN Review* 22, no. 1 (fall 1994): 51–55.

Smith, A. "Walter Dean Myers." *Publishers Weekly* 239 (July 20, 1992): 217–18.

Sutton, Roger. "Threads in Our Cultural Fabric." *School Library Journal* 40, no. 6 (June 1994): 24–28.

Awards and Prizes

Coretta Scott King Award, 1989

Margaret A. Edwards Award, 1994

100 All-Star Choices for Teens, 2000

Popular Paperbacks, YALSA, 1998

School Library Journal Best Book, 1998

Book

Bishop, Rudine Sims. *Presenting Walter Dean Myers.* Boston: Twayne Publishers, 1990.

Challenges

Challenged, but retained in the Arlington (Tex.) school district's junior high school libraries in 2000 despite a parent's complaint that the book's content was too strong for younger students.

Removed from the Laton (Calif.) Unified School District in 1999 because the novel contains violence and profanity.

Removed as required reading in the Livonia (Mich.) public schools in 1999 because it contains "too many swear words."

Challenged, but retained at the Lakewood (Ohio) High School in 1997. The book was challenged by parents who objected to its violence and vulgar language.

Removed from a twelfth-grade English class in Middleburg Heights (Ohio) in 1995 after a parent complained of its sexually explicit language.

Challenged at the West Chester (Pa.) schools in 1994.

Restricted as supplemental classroom reading material at the Jackson County (Ga.) High School in 1992 because of undesirable language and sensitive material.

Challenged in the Bluffton (Ohio) schools in 1990 because of its use of profane language.

Internet

Biographical information about Walter Dean Myers and his writing.

> http://www.scils.rutgers.edu/~kvander/myers.html

Study guides and notes for "Fallen Angels"

> http://www.antistudy.com/guides/Fallen_Angels.php

Reviews

Booklist 84 (April 15, 1988): 1419.

Bulletin of the Center for Children's Books 41 (April 1988): 118.

Horn Book 64 (July 1988): 503.

Kirkus Reviews 56 (May 1, 1988): 696.

New York Times Book Review, January 22, 1989, p. 29.

School Library Journal 34 (June 1988): 118.

Voice of Youth Advocates 11 (August 1998): 133.

Forever

New York: Bradbury, 1975

High school seniors Katherine and Michael fall in love and declare they will love each other forever. Their story is a gradual progression of increased sexual activity. They fall in love quickly after meeting at a party. During several months they share their first kiss, various stages of fondling, and then sexual intercourse. They marvel at their love for one another, and Katherine visits Planned Parenthood in New York City for birth control pills.

Their friends, Artie and Erica, play out a brief drama in the background. Artie, who is already a talented actor, commits suicide after Erica leaves him. Another friend, Sybil, who is sexually promiscuous, has a baby and gives her up for adoption.

Katherine and Michael are both distressed to be separated during the summer, since they know they will be leaving for different colleges in the fall. Katherine works in a summer camp as an assistant tennis coach, while Michael works in South Carolina for his brother. Katherine is horrified when her parents force her to take the job. At first Katherine writes to Michael every day, but then she becomes attracted to Theo, the tennis coach, and she is unsure of her feelings for Michael. When Michael makes a surprise visit to the camp, they break up. Michael is angry and hateful; Katherine is sad and confused. Later in the school year, they see one another and speak politely to each other. When Katherine returns to her house, she has a phone call from Theo.

Articles

Forman, Jack. "Young Adult Books: 'Watch out for #1.'" *Horn Book* 61 (January/February 1985): 85.

McNulty, Faith. "Children's Books for Christmas." *New Yorker* 59 (Dec. 5, 1983): 191.

Maynard, Joyce. "Coming of Age with Judy Blume." *New York Times Magazine*, Dec. 3, 1978, p. 80+.

Thompson, Susan. "Images of Adolescence: Part I." *Signal* 34 (1981): 5759.

Award

Margaret A. Edwards Award, 1996.

Book

Lee, Betsy. *Judy Blume's Story.* Minneapolis: Dillon, 1981.

Challenges

The book was banned from middle school libraries in the Elgin (Ill.) School District U46 in 1997 because of its sex scenes. The decision was upheld in June 1999 after an hour of emotional school board discussion.

Challenged at the Wilton (Iowa) School District for junior and senior high school students in 1996 because of its sexual content.

Removed from the Fort Clarke Middle School Library in Gainesville (Fla.) in 1995 after a science teacher objected to its sexually explicit content and a reference to marijuana.

Restricted to a reserve section of the Delta High School Library in Muncie (Ind.) in 1995. Parents must give their permission in writing before their children can check out the book.

Removed from Mediapolis (Iowa) School District libraries in 1994 because it "does not promote abstinence and monogamous relationships [and] lacks any aesthetic, literary, or social value." Returned to shelves a month later, but accessible only to high schoolers.

Placed on the "parental permission shelf" at the Rib Lake (Wis.) High School Library in 1993 after Superintendent Ray Parks filed a "request for reconsideration" because he found the book "sexually explicit." It was subsequently confiscated by the high school principal that year. A federal jury in Madison, Wis., awarded $394,560 to a former Rib Lake High School guidance counselor after finding that his contract was not renewed in retaliation for speaking out against the district's book policy. The counselor had criticized the decision of the Rib Lake High School principal to restrict student access to the novel.

Removed from the Frost Junior High School Library in Schaumburg (Ill.) in 1993 because "it's basically a sexual 'how-to-do' book for junior high students. It glamorizes [sex] and puts ideas in their heads."

Placed on reserve at the Herrin (Ill.) Junior High School Library in 1992 and can be checked out only with a parent's written permission because the novel is "sexually provocative reading."

The West Hernando (Fla.) Middle School principal recommended in 1988 that Blume's novel be removed from school shelves because it is "inappropriate."

Challenged at the Marshwood Junior High School classroom library in Eliot (Maine) in 1987 because the "book does not paint a responsible role of parents"; its "cast of sex-minded teenagers is not typical of high schoolers today"; and the "pornographic sexual exploits (in the book) are unsuitable for junior high school role models."

Challenged at the Moreno Valley (Calif.) Unified School District libraries in 1987 because it "contains profanity, sexual situations, and themes that allegedly encourage disrespectful behavior."

Challenged at the Campbell County (Wyo.) school libraries in 1986 because it is "pornographic" and would encourage young readers "to experiment with sexual encounters."

Placed on a restricted shelf by the Patrick County (Va.) School Board in 1986.

Challenged at the Cedar Rapids (Iowa) Public Library in 1984 because it is "pornography and explores areas God didn't intend to explore outside of marriage."

Challenged and eventually moved from the Holdredge (Nebr.) Public Library's young adult section to the adult section in 1984 because the "book is pornographic and does not promote the sanctity of family life."

Challenged at the Howard-Suamico (Wis.) High School in 1983 because "it demoralizes marital sex." Challenged at the Akron (Ohio) School District libraries in 1983.

Challenged at the Orlando (Fla.) schools in 1982. Challenged in 1982 at the Park Hill (Mo.) South Junior High School Library, where it was housed on restricted shelves because the book promotes "the stranglehold of humanism on life in America."

Challenged at the Midvalley Junior-Senior High School in Scranton (Pa.) in 1982 because it contains "four-letter words and talked about masturbation, birth control, and disobedience to parents."

Internet

Educational Paperback Association, Author Biographies: Judy Blume

http://www.edupaperback.org/authorbios/Blume_Judy.html

January Magazine, January Interview: Judy Blume

http://www.januarymagazine.com/profiles/blume.html

Judy Blume's Home Base: The Official Site

http://www.judyblume.com

Scholastic Authors Online: Judy Blume

http://teacher.scholastic.com/authorsandbooks/authors/blume/bio.htm

Teachers@Random, Authors/Illustrators: Judy Blume

http://www.randomhouse.com/teachers/authors/blum.html

Reviews

Booklist 72 (Oct. 15, 1975): 291.

Bulletin of the Center for Children's Books 29 (March 1976): 106.

Children's Literature in Education 20 (June 1989): 81.

English Journal 65 (March 1976): 90.

English Journal 66 (January 1977): 64.

English Journal 67 (May 1978): 90.

Horn Book 61 (January 1985): 86.

Kirkus Reviews 43 (Oct. 1, 1975): 1136.

Mother Jones 5 (January 1980): 60.

Ms. 16 (August 1987): 160.

New Statesman 92 (Nov. 5, 1976): 644.

New York Times Book Review, Dec. 28, 1975, p. 20.

Publishers Weekly 208 (Aug. 18, 1975): 63.

School Librarian 32 (September 1984): 209.

Times Literary Supplement, Oct. 1, 1976, p. 1238.

Top of the News 37 (fall 1980): 57.

Videos

Children's Author: Judy Blume. NBC-TV, 1980. 15 minutes.

Forever. CBS-TV, 1978.

ANONYMOUS

Go Ask Alice

Englewood Cliffs, N.J.: Prentice Hall, 1971

Alice (not her real name) is excited about the impending move her family will make. In her early diary entries she notes that this is a chance for her to begin her life anew. Her father, a college professor, has taken a new teaching post, and Alice and her brother Tim and sister Alex are packed and ready to go. Alice finds it tough at first to make friends in her new school. Finally, she meets Beth, and the two become good friends quickly. However, summer vacation means separation, so Alice decides that rather than moping around the house, she will go spend part of her summer with her grandparents. There she meets some old acquaintances from her old high school. She attends a party with some former classmates where she is slipped LSD. Alice discovers that she enjoys the wild and free sensations she has while high on acid and tries it again. Drugs seem to give Alice the independence and freedom she lacks; she even has her first sexual experience while high.

When Alice returns home at the end of the summer, she has problems adjusting to the boring routine. She can't sleep, can't seem to function normally. A doctor prescribes sleeping pills and tranquilizers and, before long, Alice is addicted to these pills. She meets a young woman named Chris while shopping one day. Chris introduces Alice to the world of speed (amphetamines) and pot. Alice's parents become concerned about her behavioral changes, but there is little they can do. Alice and Chris date two young men who convince them to sell drugs to support their own habits. Chris and Alice know they must escape from this situation, so they run away to San Francisco vowing never to do drugs again. It is not long before the drug scene beckons, however, and Alice and Chris find out the hard way that people will do anything for drugs. They return to their families, each wanting a fresh start in life, a life without drugs.

Sobriety is difficult for Alice and Chris. They want to avoid their old friends, the ones with whom they did drugs. However, once the girls return to school, they discover that people are unwilling to believe they are clean. They are approached by classmates seeking drugs and older pushers who threaten them with harm. Once more, Alice and Chris run away from home.

Alice returns home once more, determined to stay clean. She meets Joel one day while doing research at the local college library. Joel is a wonderful young man, and the two quickly develop a close friendship. Perhaps with Joel's love and support, Alice can make a break from her past. It is not long before Alice once more sinks into the drug scene as she is tricked into taking acid. Family problems add to Alice's inability to cope. Her grandmother dies, and Alice spirals out of control in an LSD flashback. She is institutionalized in a mental hospital for a while and finally released to rejoin her family. It seems her life is back on track. Alice's diary ends abruptly. An editor's note indicates that Alice died of undetermined causes.

Articles

Bosmajian, Hamida. "Tricks of the Text and Acts of Reading by Censors and Adolescents." *Children's Literature in Education* 18, no. 2 (summer 1987): 89–96.

Isaacs, Kathleen T. "*Go Ask Alice:* What Middle Schoolers Choose to Read." *New Advocate* 5, no. 2 (spring 1992): 129–43.

Peck, Richard. "In the Country of Teenage Fiction." *American Libraries* 4 (April 1973): 204–7.

Awards and Prizes

Best of the Best Books for Young Adults, 1970–1983

Christopher Book Award, 1972

Media and Methods Maxi Award for Best Paperback, 1973

100 All-Star Choices for Teens, 2000

Popular Paperbacks, YALSA, 2000

Still Alive: The Best of the Best Books for Young Adults, 1960–1974

Challenges

Removed from the Aledo (Tex.) Middle School library in 1999 and restricted at the high school library to students with parental permission. A parent complained about the book's references to drug use, vulgar language, and descriptions of sex.

Confiscated by a Tiverton (R.I.) middle school principal in 1998, while the class was reading it. The book was later returned by the school board.

Banned from the Jonathan Alder School District in Plain City (Ohio) in 1995; and challenged at the Houston Junior and Senior High School in Wasilla (Ark.) that year. Removed from a supplemental reading list for sophomore English students in Warm Springs (Va.) in 1995 because of its "profanity and indecent situations."

Banned from a ninth-grade reading list at Shepherd Hill High School in Dudley (Mass.) in 1994 because of "gross and vulgar language and graphic description of drug use and sexual conduct."

Removed from an English class in Buckhannon-Upshur (W.Va.) High School in 1993 because of numerous obscenities.

Removed from the Wall Township (N.J.) Intermediate School library in 1993 by the superintendent of schools because the book contains "inappropriate" language and "borders on pornography." The superintendent had originally ordered the book removed from all reading lists and classroom book collections in 1987. "I thought we'd got rid of them all about five years ago," he explained in 1993.

Challenged at the King Middle School in Portland (Maine) in 1988.

Challenged at the Central Gwinnett (Ga.) High School library in 1987 because "it encourages students to steal and to take drugs."

Removed from the middle school library shelves in Kalkaska (Mich.) in 1986 because the book contains "objectionable language."

The Gainsville (Ga.) Public Library in 1986 prohibited young readers from checking out this book along with forty others. The books, on subjects ranging from hypnosis and drug abuse to breast-feeding and sexual dysfunction, are kept in a locked room.

Challenged at the Rankin County (Miss.) School District in 1984 because it is "profane and sexually questionable."

Challenged at the Osseo School District in Brooklyn Park (Minn.) in 1983, when a school board member found the book's language "personally offensive."

Challenged in Pagosa Springs (Colo.) schools in 1983 because a parent objected to the "graphic language, subject matter, immoral tone, and lack of literary quality found in the book."

Challenged at the Safety Harbor Middle School Library in St. Petersburg (Fla.) in 1982, where written parental permission was required to check out the title.

Removed from the school library in North Bergen (N.J.) in 1980 due to "objectionable" language and explicit sex scenes. Removed from the school libraries in Eagle Pass, Tex. (1977); Trenton, N.J. (1977); Saginaw, Mich. (1975); Levit-town, N.Y. (1975); and Kalamazoo, Mich. (1974).

Reviews

Booklist 68 (Sept. 15, 1998): 181.

English Journal 62 (January 1973): 146.

Kirkus Reviews 39 (July 15, 1971): 776.

Library Journal 97 (March 15, 1972): 1174.

Publishers Weekly 201 (March 27, 1972): 80.

School Library Journal 18 (July 1998): 122.

JANET BODE and STAN MACK

Heartbreak and Roses: Real Life Stories of Troubled Love

New York: Delacorte, 1994

This nonfiction look at love gone wrong is told from the points of view of twelve teenagers. Their stories could serve as a template for a wide variety of teens who encounter problems with love. In addition to the stories of the twelve teens, Bode and Mack include a scattering of fact boxes with statistics about teens and their relationships. An appendix provides resources for teen and adult readers.

In the first vignette, we meet Bonnie and Michael, who dated until Michael became physically abusive. Michael was nice at first, but then he began to pressure her to have sex. Ultimately, Michael tried to prevent Bonnie from seeing any of her friends. He threatened to kill himself if they were to break up. After their breakup, Bonnie continued to find it difficult to trust other boys. Bonnie worries that all boys will treat her with the same contempt.

Maura and Louis should be perfect for one another as Maura is thirteen and a flirt just like Louis. Louis falls in love with Maura, but she is attracted to other boys. Though Louis pursues her, Maura continues to resist becoming exclusive. Pam is fifteen and has no boyfriend. Her girlfriends are also nonexistent. As a matter of fact, one has died recently, leaving a hole in Pam's life. One night Pam decides to lose her virginity. She barely knows the young man with whom she sleeps. There are other sexual partners after this one.

Eventually, Pam decides that this type of relationship is not a good idea.

Ofelia wants to be close to her boyfriend, Antoine. The situation is complicated because Antoine is African-American. Ofelia is Caucasian and partly disabled from a severe car accident. Once Ofelia and Antoine decide to become intimate, they must plan contraception and deal with the other details. Another vignette, told in comic strip-type format, discusses the relationship between Kirsten, who is fourteen, and Curtis, who is seventeen. Curtis visits Kirsten when she is babysitting. He tells her all about himself, including the fact that he is a skinhead. When Kirsten gets pregnant, her parents want her to have an abortion. Instead, Kirsten and Curtis run away and live on the streets for a while. Eventually, the two return home and make plans to marry.

Seth is sixteen and has very strict parents. He sneaks out of the house and meets another boy named Zach. Seth is confused about his feelings toward Zach, which are more than those of a friend. Is it okay to feel this way about another boy? Is what he feels real? Charlene and Forrest are both living in a homeless shelter when they meet and begin to develop a relationship. Charlene and her mother are forced to move to a new location, and Charlene realizes that maintaining a long-distance relationship is quite difficult.

Charlene attempts suicide, and Forrest ends up in jail.

Suki is eighteen. Her father is on drugs and her mother is physically abusive. Suki herself was raped when she was sixteen. When she becomes attracted to a young man, she wants to wait before taking their relationship to the sexual level. The following vignette is also in comic strip format. Yoelyne wants desperately to have a boyfriend. She even lies about having one because she wants so much to be loved.

At fifteen, Eric has never even kissed a girl. He is attracted to Michelle, but ends up taking Liza to a dance. The two become close, but their relationship is forbidden by both sets of parents. In the final story, seventeen-year-old Amy begins dating a new guy at her school named Waylon. The two break up when the relationship gets too serious too quickly. Amy is hurt when Waylon refuses to remain friends and even goes so far as to call her names after their separation.

Awards and Prizes

Best Books for Young Adults, 1995
Popular Paperbacks, YALSA, 2000

Challenge

The book was pulled from the Ouachita Parish school library in Monroe (La.) in 1996 because of its sexual content. The Louisiana chapter of the ACLU filed a lawsuit in the federal courts on Oct. 3, 1996, claiming that the principal and the school superintendent violated First Amendment free speech rights and also failed to follow established procedures when they removed the book. The three-year-old case headed to court after the Ouachita Parish School Board made no decision to seek a settlement at a special meeting on April 12, 1999. On Aug. 17, 1999, the Ouachita Parish School Board agreed to return the book to the library and to develop a new book-selection policy that follows state guidelines for school media programs.

Internet

Obituary and tribute to Janet Bode and her work

  http://www.stirlinglaw.com/asg/
  janbode.htm

Reviews

Booklist 90 (Oct. 1, 1994): 315.
Bulletin of the Center for Children's Books 47 (September 1994): 6.
School Library Journal 40 (July 1994): 116.

I Know Why The Caged Bird Sings

New York: Random House, 1970

As the book opens, Maya (a childhood name coined by her brother, who called Marguerite "mya sister") and her brother Bailey have just been sent to Stamps, Ark., to live with their paternal grandmother following the divorce of their parents. Visits by the Ku Klux Klan, lynchings, and racism are all commonplace to young Maya. As a matter of fact, she regards entering the white section of town as entering "enemy territory." There is always a chance that harm will come to her there. Maya watches from the porch of the store run by her grandmother, and sees poor white girls mock and humiliate her grandmother. Though Maya is filled with rage, she can do nothing to come to her grandmother's defense. In that desperate moment, Maya sees the strength of the elderly woman she calls "Momma." Church offers no respite for Maya and her brother, who are forced to sit in the front of the church and behave as models for the other children.

It is almost a relief when the children's father shows up to take them to St. Louis. There they will meet their mother for the first time since the divorce. However, the new living situation places Maya in even more danger. Her mother has a live-in boyfriend named Mr. Freeman who begins molesting Maya shortly after her arrival. Freeman threatens to kill Bailey if Maya utters one word about their special relationship. When Freeman's molestation becomes rape, however, Maya is forced to testify against him in court. After the trial, Mr. Freeman is found beaten to death. Maya and Bailey are sent back to Stamps to live.

Once back in Arkansas, Maya is befriended by Mrs. Flowers, who begins to teach Maya about the importance of learning. Though reading and writing and speaking take on new dimensions, Maya's life is still rather mundane. She still encounters racism: a white dentist refuses to treat her even in an emergency, and at her eighth-grade graduation the speaker notes only athletes as heroes of the black community.

Maya again leaves Stamps with her father and travels to Mexico. There she lives with him and his girlfriend. It is an uncomfortable living arrangement, and one day Maya is stabbed by her father's girlfriend. She leaves the house and winds up living in an abandoned car for thirty days. Eventually, Maya makes her way back to her mother, who is now married to Mr. Clidell in California. Maya yearns to work on the streetcars in San Francisco, but she is denied employment simply because she is black. However, she perseveres and fights to obtain a job. Maya also finishes school. Deciding that she wants to "become a woman," she plans an elaborate seduction of a neighborhood man. Soon Maya learns that she is pregnant. Her son is born, and this installment of her story comes to an end.

Article

Rochman, Hazel. "The Courage of
   Ordinary Life." *School Library
   Journal* 30, no. 7 (January 1984):
   42–43.

Awards and Prizes

Best Books for Young Adults, 1970

Best of the Best Books for Young Adults,
   1970–1983

Best of the Best Books for Young Adults,
   1994

100 All-Star Choices for Teens, 2000

Still Alive: The Best of the Best Books for
   Young Adults, 1960–1974

Challenges

The book was challenged on the
Poolesville (Miss.) High School's reading
list in 2000 due to its sexual content and
language.

Removed from the seventh- and eighth-
grade reading list at Unity (N.H.)
Elementary School in 1999 because the
book "is too sexually explicit." Banned
from the school library and classrooms of
the Delores Parrott Middle School in
Brooksville (Fla.) in 1998. Removed from
the Turrentine Middle School's reading
list in Alamance (N.C.) that same year.

Removed from the ninth-grade English
curriculum in Anne Arundel County
(Md.) in 1998 by the school superintendent after parents complained that the
book "portrays white people as being
horrible, nasty, stupid people." Returned
to the approved reading list.

Removed from the reading list of the
Lakota High School in Union Township
(Ohio) in 1997 because of Angelou's brief
description of being raped at age eight
and other sexual content. In 1997 the
book was retained in the Mukilteo
(Wash.) high school; challenged at the
Folsom Cordova (Calif.) school district;
removed from the curriculum at the
Turrentine (N.C.) middle school; and
challenged as an advanced-placement
English class reading assignment in
Wayne County (Ga.), with all these challenges based on the book's sexually
explicit passages.

Challenged (but retained) on an
optional reading list at the East Lawrence
High School in Moulton (Ala.) in 1996
because the superintendent decided "the
poet's descriptions of being raped as a
young girl were pornographic." Retained
on the Round Rock (Tex.) high school
reading lists in 1996 after a challenge that
the book was too violent.

Removed from the curriculum in the
Gilbert (Ariz.) Unified Schools in 1995
pending a review of its contents.
Complaining parents said the book did
not represent "traditional values."
Challenged, but retained in the Volusia
County (Fla.) schools in 1995 after complaints that it is "sexually explicit and
promotes cohabitation and rape."
Removed from Southwood High School
in Caddo Parish (La.) in 1995 because the
book's language and content were objectionable. Eventually, the book was
returned after students petitioned and
demonstrated against the action. The
book was challenged at the Carroll
School in Southlake (Tex.) in 1995
because it was deemed "pornographic"
and full of "gross evils."

Challenged, but retained as required
reading for all of Dowling High School's
sophomores in Des Moines (Iowa) in
1994. Challenged as part of the
Ponderosa High School curriculum in
Castle Rock (Colo.) in 1994 because it is
a "lurid tale of sexual perversion."

Challenged at Westwood High School in Austin (Tex.) in 1994. The superintendent later ruled that parents must first give permission for their children to be taught potentially controversial literature.

Parents in Haines City (Fla.) in 1993 petitioned the Polk County School Board to ban the book from the high school because of the rape scene. The review committee said that the objections to the book were related as much or more to the author's race as to the book's content and declined to ban the book.

Temporarily banned from the Caledonia Middle School in Columbus (Miss.) in 1993 on the grounds that it is too sexually explicit to be read by children.

Challenged at Amador Valley High School in Pleasanton (Calif.) in 1992 because of sexually explicit language.

Removed from a Banning (Calif.) eighth-grade class in 1991 after several parents complained about explicit passages involving child molestation and rape.

Rejected as required reading for a gifted ninth-grade English class in Bremerton (Wash.) in 1990 because of the book's "graphic" description of molestation.

Challenged at Mount Abram Regional High School in Strong (Maine) in 1988 because parents objected to the rape scene.

In 1983 four members of the Alabama State Textbook Committee called for the book's rejection because Angelou's work "preaches bitterness and hatred against whites."

Internet

Frequently Asked Questions for Maya Angelou

http://www.math.buffalo.edu/~sww/angelou/angelou.bio.bib.html

Interview with Maya Angelou by David Frost

http://www.newsun.com/angelou.html

Official Maya Angelou Web Site

http://www.mayaangelou.com/

Reviews

American Libraries 1 (July 1970): 714.

Booklist 66 (June 15, 1970): 1256.

English Journal 80 (December 1991): 26.

Kirkus Reviews 37 (Dec. 15, 1969): 1330.

Library Journal 95 (March 15, 1970): 1018.

New York Times, Feb. 25, 1970, p. 45.

Publishers Weekly 196 (Dec. 29, 1969): 64.

School Library Journal 30 (January 1984): 42.

Killing Mr. Griffin

Boston: Little, Brown, 1978

Students in Mr. Griffin's senior English class think he is too strict and is unfair in his grading practices, mainly because he doesn't accept late papers. Jeff Garrett, a basketball player, and Dave Ruggles, president of the senior class, receive F's on assignments, no matter what their excuses are for not turning in the papers on time. One of their classmates, Mark McKinney, is repeating senior English because he failed it last year. He mumbles, "That Griffin's the sort of guy you'd like to kill." Mark suggests they plan to kidnap Mr. Griffin just to scare him and show him that he can't treat students with such contempt. Jeff, Dave, and Betsy, a senior with a crush on Mark, are reluctant at first but agree to Mark's plan to kidnap Mr. Griffin. They convince Susan McConnell, an insecure, conscientious student, to help them lure Mr. Griffin into a trap.

The boys attack Mr. Griffin in his own car, force a bag over his head, and wind rope around his body. They drive him to a remote location away from the city where they had recently picnicked. Betsy finds a vial of Mr. Griffin's nitroglycerin pills for "pain of angina," but Mark crushes them. The students leave the teacher tied up but expect to return at midnight after the basketball game to release him. When Susan discovers that Mr. Griffin has been left there, she convinces Dave to come with her to let Mr. Griffin go. To Susan's horror Mr. Griffin is not asleep, but dead. Later that night the boys bury him where he died.

In the meantime Mr. Griffin's wife reports him missing and offers a $1,000 reward for any information leading to his location. The students are questioned by the police, and there are problems. The police find the body, and only a few dollars and Mr. Griffin's Stanford class ring are missing. Dave took the ring and his grandmother has it. Mark goes to Dave's house and kills the grandmother to get the ring. Susan continues to want to report Mr. Griffin's death to the police, but the others talk her out of it. The autopsy report shows that he died of coronary arrest, possibly preceded by a severe angina attack. Mark, Jeff, and Betsy go to Susan's house, tie her up, and Mark stays behind to set the house on fire and thus silence Susan and her threats to tell what happened to Mr. Griffin and to Dave's grandmother. Before the house can burn, however, Mrs. Griffin and Detective Baca show up, catch Mark, and save Susan. Mark, who fits the clinical description of a psychopath, faces three trials. Jeff, Dave, and Betsy are charged with second-degree murder. If Susan will tell the truth about the events, turning state's evidence against the others, she can avoid a manslaughter charge.

Articles

Duncan, Lois. "1992 Margaret A. Edwards Award Acceptance Speech."

Journal of Youth Services in Libraries 6 (winter 1993): 108–12.

Overstreet, D. W. "Help, Help! An Analysis of Female Victims in the Novels of Lois Duncan." *ALAN Review* 21 (spring 1994): 43–45.

Sutton, R. "A Conversation with Lois Duncan." *School Library Journal* 38 (June 1992): 20.

Awards and Prizes

Best Books for Young Adults, 1978

Best of the Best Books for Young Adults: 1970–1983

Here We Go Again: 25 Years of Best Books: Selections from 1967 to 1992

Margaret A. Edwards Award, 1992

Nothin' But the Best: Best of the Best Books for Young Adults, 1966–1986

Still Alive: The Best of the Best Books for Young Adults, 1960–1974

Books

Duncan, Lois. *How to Write and Sell Your Personal Experiences*. Cincinnati, Ohio: Writer's Digest, 1979.

———. *Chapters: My Growth as a Writer*. Boston: Little, Brown, 1982.

Challenges

The book was challenged in a Bristol (Pa.) middle school for violence and language in 2000.

Challenged in the Shenandoah Valley (Pa.) Junior-Senior High School curriculum in 1995 because of violence, strong language, and unflattering references to God.

Pulled from a Bonsall (Calif.) middle school eighth-grade reading list in 1992 because of violence and profanity.

Challenged at the Sinnott Elementary School in Milpitas (Calif.) in 1988 because the book contains "needlessly foul" language and has no "redeeming qualities."

Internet

Teachers@Random, Authors/Illustrators: Lois Duncan

http://www.randomhouse.com/teachers/authors/dunc.html

Reviews

Best Sellers 38 (August 1978): 154.

Book Watch 12 (March 1991): 12.

Booklist 74 (March 1, 1978): 1092.

Booklist 86 (May 1, 1990): 1696.

Booklist 90 (April 1, 1994): 1462.

Bulletin of the Center for Children's Books 32 (October 1978): 27.

Horn Book 54 (August 1978): 400.

Kirkus Reviews 46 (May 1, 1978): 500.

Kliatt Young Adult Paperback Book Guide 14 (winter 1980): 6.

New York Times Book Review, April 30, 1978, p. 54.

Publishers Weekly 213 (Feb. 20, 1978): 127.

Publishers Weekly 216 (Aug. 27, 1979): 385.

School Library Journal 24 (May 1978): 86.

School Library Journal 27 (November 1980): 47.

Voice of Youth Advocates 14 (April 1991): 72

Video

A Visit with Lois Duncan. Albuquerque, N.Mex.: RDA Enterprises, 1985.

The Outsiders

New York: Viking, 1966

At age fourteen, Ponyboy should be enjoying high school. He is a decent student who loves to read books. But finding a good book is the least of Ponyboy's troubles. He is the youngest of three brothers. Their parents died years ago in an accident, so older brother Darry has assumed the position of head of the household. Pony's other brother, Soda, dropped out of school and now works as a mechanic in a garage. As a "greaser," Pony must be careful not to encroach on the territory of the more well-to-do students. The Socs (short for "socials") take offense if someone from the wrong side of the tracks, like Ponyboy and the other Greasers, crosses the line which separates the two groups. At a drive-in movie one night, Ponyboy and his friend Johnny run into Cherry and Marcia. This seemingly inconsequential incident sets off a chain of events which leads to tragedy.

Ponyboy and Johnny linger outside after the movie has ended. When Ponyboy arrives home past his curfew, Darry hits him. Pony decides to run away from home and heads back to find Johnny. Before the two boys can get away, they are jumped by a car full of Socs. In the skirmish, Johnny stabs and kills one of the Socs. Now the two boys know they must flee for their lives. No one will believe that a Greaser had to kill a Soc in self-defense. With the aid of some of their Greaser friends, Johnny and Pony head off to an abandoned church far from their town. They hole up there until someone can get word to them that the coast is clear.

After a week, Dally and Two-Bit come to visit Johnny and Pony. When the boys return to the abandoned church, a fire has broken out. Several children are trapped inside the burning building, and Johnny, Dally, and Pony manage to rescue them. Pony's injuries are minor, but Johnny's back is broken when the flaming roof collapses on him. Johnny, Pony, and Dally are rushed to the hospital and hailed as heroes. However, life is still complicated by the death of the Soc and the plans for a rumble between the two gangs. Though the Greasers win the fight and regain control of their turf, the victory is short-lived when Johnny dies. Johnny's death weighs heavily on Dally, who confronts a policeman while waving an unloaded pistol, deliberately provoking the police into shooting him. Pony is devastated by these losses. His only solace may come by writing about Johnny and Dally and the other Greasers he calls family.

Articles

Foster, Harold. M. "A Book, A Place, A Time: Using Young Adult Novels in a Reading Workshop." *English Journal* 84, no. 5 (September 1995): 115–19.

"The Novels of S. E. Hinton: Springboard to Personal Growth for Adolescents." *Adolescence* 22 (fall 1987): 642–46.

Peck, Richard. "In the Country of Teenage Fiction." *American Libraries* 4 (April 1973): 204–7.

Robin, Lisa. "S. E. Hinton Knows How to Write for the Young and the Restless." *Media and Methods* 18 (June–July 1982): 28.

Tighe, Mary Ann, and Charles Avinger. "Teaching Tomorrow's Classics." *ALAN Review* 21, no. 3 (spring 1994): 9–13.

Awards and Prizes

Best Books for Young Adults, 1975

Margaret A. Edwards Award, first recipient, 1988

Massachusetts Children's Book Award, 1979

Nothin' But the Best: Best of the Best Books for Young Adults, 1966–1986

100 All-Star Choices for Teens, 2000

Still Alive: The Best of the Best Books for Young Adults, 1960–1974

Book

Daly, Jay. *Presenting S. E. Hinton.* Boston: Twayne Publishers, 1987.

Challenges

The book was challenged at the George Washington Middle School in Eleanor (W.Va.) in 2000 due to objections to its focus on gangs and gang fights.

A complaint was filed in the Boone (Iowa) school district in 1992 against the book for glamorizing smoking and drinking and its excessive violence and use of obscenities.

Banned from classroom use in Panama City (Fla.) in 1987 by the school superintendent for "profanity" and "a lot of vulgar language."

Challenged in Milwaukee (Wis.) in 1987 for being "too negative," for portraying drug and alcohol abuse, and for depicting characters from broken homes.

Challenged on an eighth-grade reading list in South Milwaukee (Wis.) in 1986 because "drug and alcohol use are common" in the book.

Internet

Official S. E. Hinton Web Site
  http://www.sehinton.com/

Other Resources

The Outsiders. Motion picture. Directed by Francis Ford Coppola. Warner Brothers/Zoetrope Studios, 1983.

Reviews

Booklist 64 (Oct. 1, 1967): 176.

Horn Book 43 (August 1967): 475.

Journal of Reading 22 (November 1978): 126.

Kirkus Reviews 35 (April 15, 1967): 506.

Library Journal 92 (May 15, 1967): 2028.

School Library Journal 36 (December 1990): 30.

STEPHEN CHBOSKY

The Perks of Being a Wallflower

New York: Pocket Books/Simon and Schuster, 1999

Charlie is a high school freshman who keeps a journal that chronicles his journey from loner and introvert to a person with friends and increased self-confidence. His gradual emergence into a social being includes both pain and joy. Fifteen-year-old Charlie meets Sam and Patrick, both seniors, at a football game and immediately develops a crush on beautiful Sam. This stepsister and stepbrother pair become his first high school friends. Throughout his freshman year Charlie observes the behavior of other people, experiences the ups and downs of a teenager's life, and records his reflections about his world with intelligence and freshness.

From his older sister Susan he learns about the agonies of young love. Susan falls in love with a boy who hit her. When her parents find out what he did, they forbid Susan to see him. Susan ignores their warnings and proceeds to fall deeper in love with him. Charlie even witnesses some of their lovemaking sessions. After Charlie gets his driver's license, he finds out that she's pregnant and he takes her to a clinic to get an abortion.

How to cope with sexual relationships continues to occupy Charlie's mind and body. From Patrick he learns the pleasures of masturbation. At a party one night he inadvertently witnesses a boy raping a girl. Then he's surprised to see Patrick kissing Brad, one of the football players. Sexual fantasies occupy some of Charlie's dreams about Sam, which he finds embarrassing. Mary Elizabeth becomes Charlie's girlfriend, and they engage in a heavy petting session, but he doesn't really enjoy her company. She talks too much and doesn't listen enough.

Charlie has a few brief encounters with drugs. He unwittingly takes LSD at a party. He smokes ten cigarettes a day, and sometimes smokes pot.

Despite his reluctance to participate in life, his freshman year is peppered with friendly encounters. From Bill, a first-year teacher, Charlie learns that he has writing talent and a rare intelligence. Charlie also learns from Bill that at least a few adults are kind and understanding and can be trusted. His growing friendships with Sam, Patrick, and Mary Elizabeth involve the Rocky Horror Show, Secret Santas, dancing, parties, and companionable car rides.

Charlie sees a psychiatrist on a regular basis, but the reader doesn't realize why he needs one until the end of the book. It turns out that Charlie's dead, beloved Aunt Helen molested him for many years. He reaches a crisis when he begins remembering. He is in the hospital for two months and this time he answers all the psychiatrist's questions about his Aunt Helen. At the end of this coming-of-age novel Charlie is looking forward to tomorrow, the first day of his sophomore year. This year he's not afraid and even thinks he can "participate" in life.

Challenge

Removed from a summer preparation course at Newton (Mass.) High School in 2001 after a parent's complaint that the book contains sexually explicit paragraphs.

Internet

Borders.com Presents Steve Chbosky
http://www.talkcity.com/transcripts/borders/3-05-1999.1-1.htmpl

Reviews

Booklist 95 (Feb. 15, 1999): 1038.

Booklist 96 (Nov. 15, 1999): 616.

Booklist 97 (June 1/June 15, 2001): 1863.

Publishers Weekly 246 (Jan. 25, 1999): 73.

School Library Journal 45 (June 1999): 126.

Time 154 (July 19, 1999): 79.

USA Today, April 9, 1999, p. 13E.

Wall Street Journal-Eastern Edition, July 27, 2001, p. W13.

The Pigman

New York: Harper and Row, 1968

In alternating chapters John Conlan and Lorraine Jensen, high school sophomores, describe their friendship with an old man, Mr. Angelo Pignati. John and Lorraine call their recitation of the events that led up to Mr. Pignati's death a "memorial epic." Adventure, love, death, family, friends, and enemies are all represented in the truth as they see it.

The Pigman, so named for his extensive collection of decorative pigs, generously shares his home, money, food, sense of fun, and his love of Bobo, a zoo baboon, but hides his wife's recent death from the teenagers.

In turn, John and Lorraine feel at home at the Pigman's house in a way they have never felt in their own homes. John's father criticizes him and compares him unfavorably with an older brother; John's mother cleans obsessively and avoids conflicts. Lorraine's mother nurses dying elderly men and complains bitterly to Lorraine about the burdens of being a single mother.

The Pigman's heart attack and his few days in the hospital give John and Lorraine free run of the Pigman's house. They have a party which ends with the Pigman arriving home a day early to find a houseful of teenagers, some broken pigs, and his dead wife's torn dress. John and Lorraine are sorry for having the party, and they convince the Pigman to meet them at the zoo to visit Bobo. On learning that Bobo died of pneumonia a few days earlier, the Pigman has another heart attack and dies in the monkey house. John and Lorraine blame themselves for his death.

Articles

Haley, Beverly A., and Kenneth L. Donelson. "Pigs and Hamburgers, Cadavers and Gamma Rays: Paul Zindel's Adolescents." *Elementary English* 51 (October 1974) 941–45.

Janecsko, Paul. "In Their Own Words, an Interview with Paul Zindel." *English Journal* 66 (October 1977): 20–21.

Lesesne, Teri. "Humor, Bathos and Fear: An Interview with Paul Zindel." *Teacher Librarian* 27 (December 1999): 60–62.

Mercier, Jean. "Paul Zindel." *Publishers Weekly* 212 (Dec. 5, 1977): 6–7.

Mertz, Maia Pank. "Enhancing Literary Understandings through Young Adult Fiction." *Publishing Research Quarterly* 8 (spring 1992): 23.

Award

Margaret A. Edwards Award, 2002

Books

Forman, Jack Jacob. *Presenting Paul Zindel*. Boston: Twayne Publishers, 1988.

Hipple, Theodore W. *A Teacher's Guide to the Novels of Paul Zindel*. New York: Bantam Books, 1988.

Zindel, Paul. "Paul Zindel on Censorship." In *Places I Never Meant to Be*, ed. Judy Blume. New York: Simon and Schuster, 1999.

Challenges

Challenged at the Lynchburg (Va.) middle and high school English classes in 1992 because the novel contains twenty-nine instances of "destructive, disrespectful, antisocial and illegal behavior . . . placed in a humorous light, making it seem acceptable."

Challenged as suitable curriculum material in the Harwinton and Burlington (Conn.) schools in 1990 because it contains profanity and subject matter that set bad examples and give students negative views of life.

Challenged at the Hillsboro (Mo.) School District in 1985 because the novel features "liars, cheaters and stealers."

Internet

Educational Paperback Association: Zindel, Paul

http://www.edupaperback.org/authorbios/Zindel_Paul.hml

Paul Zindel's Biography

http://teacher.scholastic.com/authorsandbooks/authors/zindel/bio.htm

Teachers@Random, Authors/Illustrators: Paul Zindel

http://www.randomhouse.com/teachers/authors/zind.html

Zindel, Paul. "Journey to Meet the Pigman." Online article from the ALAN Review (fall 1994).

http://scholar.lib.vt.edu/ejournals/ALAN/fall94/Zindel.html

Reviews

Booklist 88 (Feb. 15, 1992): 1101.

Booklist 90 (Oct. 1, 1993): 335.

Booklist 91 (Oct. 15, 1994): 416.

English Journal 73 (September 1983): 80.

English Journal 80 (January 1991): 50.

Journal of Reading 22 (November 1978): 129.

School Library Journal 28 (April 1982): 28.

School Library Journal 46 (January 2000): 58.

Shade's Children

New York: HarperCollins, 1997

In this science fiction story everyone above the age of fourteen disappears within seconds. The period is known as The Change. Children are bused away from their homes and kept in dormitories until their Sad Birthdays. At the age of fourteen they are sent to the Meat Factory where their brains and other body parts are used to build terrifying creatures: Myrmidons, Trackers, Wingers, Screamers, and Ferrets. These creatures are used to capture escaped children and to do the bidding of seven evil Overlords who rule the land.

Out of this misery, one ray of hope appears. A former science professor, now relegated to life within computer technology without a physical body, has established a renegade group of children in an abandoned submarine. The children call him Shade. For many of the thirty children the submarine represents the only home they have ever known.

The story focuses on four children: Ella, Drum, Ninde, and Gold-Eye. These four make up a team that seeks information about the Overlords for Shade's purpose, which is to change the world back to the way it was before the disappearances. The team has dangerous encounters with the Overlords' creatures until the four young people are sent to carry out Shade's mission to destroy the radiation projector on Silver Mountain. Shade thinks that once the projector is destroyed the Overlords will disappear, the creatures will die, the children waiting in the Meat Factory and in the dorms can be freed, and they can reclaim their world.

Shade betrays the children, and gives them to the Overlords in exchange for technology to provide him with a physical body. The Overlords don't keep their part of the bargain. Ella and Drum sacrifice themselves to destroy the projector, and Ninde and Gold-Eye barely escape drowning. At the last moment Shade, a.k.a. Robert Ingram, helps rescue Ninde and Gold-Eye. The world is freed from the Overlords, Ninde and Gold-Eye grow up, and they name their children Ella and Drum in a final honor to their friends.

Articles

Gross, Melissa. "*The Giver* and *Shade's Children:* Future Views of Child Abandonment and Murder." *Children's Literature in Education* 30 (June 1999): 103.

Rolfe, Patricia. "The Nix Mix Makes Boffo Biz." *The Bulletin with Newsweek* 116 (Oct. 8, 1996): 86.

Awards and Prizes

Best Books for Young Adults, 1997
Children's Book Council Notable Book, 1997

Pick of the Lists (American Book Association), 1997

Challenge

Complaint by parents to remove the book from the Transit Middle School library in Williamsville (N.Y.) in 2001. Parents told the trustees that the book contains graphic violence, sexual innuendo, and extensive use of profanity. The school board voted 7-0 to keep the book in the library.

Internet

A Conversation with Garth Nix by Claire E. White

http://www.writerswrite.com/journal/jul00/nix.htm

Garth Nix

http://eidolon.net/garthnix

Reviews

Book Report 16 (March/April 1998): 34.

Booklist 94 (Oct. 1, 1997): 320.

Bulletin of the Center for Children's Books 51 (November 1997): 94.

Horn Book 73 (September/October 1997): 576.

Kirkus Reviews 65 (Aug. 15, 1997): 1309–10.

Publishers Weekly 244 (June 16, 1997): 60.

Reading Time (November 1997): 35.

School Library Journal 47 (August 1997): 158.

Voice of Youth Advocates 21 (June 1998): 132.

LAURIE HALSE ANDERSON

Speak

New York: Simon and Schuster, 1999

The intricate interior-monologue format of this book depicts the isolation and frustration of a young girl named Melinda who calls police to report that she has been raped at an end-of-the-school-year party which has gotten out of control. The novel, divided into four sections labeled "marking periods," relates Melinda's story in dribs and drabs. Since Melinda has no voice since the rape, most of what readers will learn must come from her reflections on events at school and from what others think, feel, and say about her.

First Marking Period

Melinda Sordino boards the school bus on her first day of high school classes wondering if anyone will sit next to her, speak to her, or even acknowledge her presence. She is an outcast, a pariah, for reasons the reader does not yet know. In the assembly that first day, Melinda meets a new student, Heather, from Ohio. Heather does not know Melinda's situation, and so the two become friends. For Melinda, each day at school is an ordeal: she is snubbed by her former best friend Rachel, has food thrown at her in the cafeteria, and is dogged in the halls by whispered taunts and threats. Ever since she called the cops on Kyle's end-of-school party last year, people torment her in mean little ways. Heather remains Melinda's only friend, but when Heather joins the Marthas (after Martha Stewart), their friendship is placed in jeopardy.

Second Marking Period

David Petrakis, Melinda's lab partner in biology class, takes on the teacher of his and Melinda's history class. Melinda admires David's ability to present his position without fear. Unfortunately, she cannot yet bring herself to speak. The only place she feels free to express herself is in Mr. Freeman's art class, where the teacher observes Melinda's pain as represented in the various drawings she makes of a tree, her semester assignment in art class. In gym class, the teacher discovers that Melinda can sink free throws with deadly accuracy. The teacher offers Melinda the chance to pass her gym class by tutoring one of the basketball players in free throwing. With a 1.7 grade point average, Melinda could never qualify to play for the basketball team because she couldn't meet the academic requirement. At this point readers learn the identity of the "monster" from Kyle's party: Andy Evans.

Third Marking Period

When Heather tells her they can no longer be friends, Melinda feels abandoned. She still cannot bring herself to speak of the awful events of the past summer. But a chance encounter with the works of Pablo Picasso in her art class has a cathartic effect on Melinda, who allows the reader to know the events which transpired at the awful end-of-the-school-year party.

Fourth Marking Period

The "beast," Andy Evans, is now flirting with Rachel, Melinda's former best friend. Rachel is planning on attending the senior prom with Andy. Melinda summons up the courage to tell Rachel what Andy did to her at the party, but Rachel refuses to believe the truth even though Melinda now knows there are others who have become Andy's victims. Rachel does break up with Andy after he makes unwanted sexual advances to her at the prom. Andy then corners Melinda in her private escape room in the school (she has commandeered an abandoned janitor closet so she can escape when things get tough in school). Melinda fights Andy off successfully. She can finally tell someone the truth about the rape. She discovers how to express her rage and fear and sorrow in her tree for Mr. Freeman's art class. Melinda has found her "voice."

Awards and Prizes

Michael L. Printz Honor Book, 2000

National Book Award finalist, 1999

School Library Journal Best Book of the Year, 1999

Challenge

Banned from an eighth-grade classroom in Arizona due to profanity, sexual content, and rape theme.

Internet

Laurie Halse Anderson's home page
http://www.writerlady.com

Reviews

Booklist 95 (Oct. 1, 1999): 247.

Bulletin of the Center for Children's Books 53 (October 1999): 45.

Horn Book 75 (September 1999): 605.

School Library Journal 45 (October 1999): 144.

The Terrorist

New York: Scholastic, 1997

Laura Williams and her family move from Boston, Mass., to London in England with Laura's father and his job, which consists of closing down factories. Her mother, her father, her eleven-year-old brother Billy, and Laura settle into a flat in a quiet neighborhood. Laura, a junior in high school, and Billy attend the London International Academy, a private school of students from diverse cultures and economic backgrounds.

Laura and Billy love living in London. Laura makes friends at school and enjoys the freedom of traveling on buses, subways, and taxis. Billy, always a whirlwind of activity, talks to everyone and anyone, collects odd things such as toilet paper and old bricks, and relishes British words and phrases. All seems to be going well with the Williams family until Billy accepts a package from a stranger.

Billy loves riding the subway to school. One morning as he hurries toward an escalator behind his two friends, a man hands Billy a package. Billy automatically takes the package and then, with a sickening realization, he knows it's a bomb. Rather than throw the deadly package away from himself and into the crowd, he hugs it. Moments later the bomb blows him apart.

After the tragedy, Laura is determined to find out who murdered her brother. She questions her fellow students relentlessly about their countries and their families. Jimmy Hopkins looks Japanese, but he's from Los Angeles; Samira, Jehran, and Mohammed are from the Middle East; Eddie's real name is Erdam Yafi. Laura's suspicions and rude questions begin to alienate her from the other students.

Oddly, one girl gravitates toward Laura. Jehran invites Laura and some other girls to a slumber party and makes an incredible request. She asks Laura for Billy's passport as a way to escape from an arranged marriage. Remarkably, Laura believes her and agrees to get Billy's passport for Jehran and help her escape to New York City. Finally, at the airport Laura realizes her mistake and stops Jehran from getting on the plane. Laura thinks she has found Billy's killer and the terrorist, but there is no real proof. At last, Laura's family is ready to leave London and return home.

Book

Carroll, Pamela Sissi. *Caroline Cooney: Faith and Fiction.* Landham, Md.: Scarecrow, 2001.

Challenges

Challenged by a seventh-grade Muslim girl at Franklin Middle School in Cedar Rapids (Iowa) in 2000. She objected to the portrayal of Muslims as terrorists.

Retained in the Cedar Rapids district middle schools and high schools.

Challenged by a seventh-grade Muslim girl at Earle B. Wood Middle School in Rockville (Md.) in 2000. She was appalled by what she saw as offensive stereotyping of Muslims. Her father complained to the teacher and principal at Wood, and then enlisted the help of the Council on American-Islamic Relations to recall the book. The book was retained.

Internet

Authors Online Library: Caroline Cooney's Biography

http://teacher.scholastic.com/ authorsandbooks/authors/cooney/

Teachers@Random, Authors/Illustrators: Caroline Cooney

http://www.randomhouse.com/teachers/ authors/caro.html

teenreads.com, Author Profile: Caroline Cooney

http://www.teenreads.com/authors/ au-cooney-caroline.asp

Reviews

Booklist 93 (July 1997): 1810.

Bulletin of the Center for Children's Books 51 (October 1997): 47.

Journal of Adolescent and Adult Literacy 41 (December 1997/January 1998): 322.

Kirkus Reviews 65 (June 1, 1997): 870.

School Library Journal 43 (September 1997): 213.

Reference Works about Authors

Authors and Artists for Young Adults. Detroit: Gale, 1989– .

Contemporary Authors. Detroit: Gale, 1967– .

Contemporary Authors, New Revision Series. Detroit: Gale, 1981– .

Contemporary Authors Autobiography Series. Detroit: Gale, 1962– .

Contemporary Literary Criticism. Detroit: Gale, 1973– .

Junior Authors and Illustrators Series. New York: H. W. Wilson, 1951– .

Major Authors and Illustrators for Children and Young Adults. Detroit: Gale, 1993– .

Something about the Author. Detroit: Gale, 1971– .

Something about the Author Autobiography. Detroit: Gale, 1986– .

Ward, M. E., et al. *Authors of Books for Young People.* 3rd ed. Metuchen, N.J.: Scarecrow, 1990.

For details about these print resources and for information about electronic sources, visit the Gale Group at http://www.galegroup.com and H. W. Wilson at http://www.hwwilson.com.

Resources Recommending Challenged Books

Best Books for Junior High Readers. Edited by John T. Gillespie. New Providence, N.J.: R. R. Bowker, 1991.

Best Books for Senior High Readers. Edited by John T. Gillespie. New Providence, N.J.: R. R. Bowker, 1991.

Best in Children's Books, 1985–90. Edited by Zena Sutherland, Betsy Hearne, and Roger Sutton. Chicago: University of Chicago Press, 1991.

Books for You: A Booklist for Senior High Students. Committee on the Senior High Booklist. NCTE Bibliography Series. Urbana, Ill.: National Council of Teachers of English, published every 3 to 5 years.

Carter, Betty. *Best Books for Young Adults: The History, the Selections, the Romance.* Chicago: American Library Association, 1994.

———. *Best Books for Young Adults.* 2nd ed. Chicago: American Library Association, 2000.

Children's Literature Review. Detroit: Gale, 1976– .

Fiction Catalog. New York: H. W. Wilson, published every 5 years with yearly supplements.

Growing Up Is Hard to Do. Edited by Sally Estes. Chicago: Booklist/American Library Association, 1994.

High-Low Handbook: Encouraging Literacy in the 1990s. 3rd ed. Compiled and edited by Ellen V. LiBretto. New York: R. R. Bowker, 1990.

Kaywell, Joan F. *Adolescents at Risk: A Guide to Fiction and Nonfiction for Young Adults, Parents and Professionals.* Westport, Conn.: Greenwood, 1993.

Middle and Junior High School Library Catalog. 8th ed. New York: H. W. Wilson, 2000.

Murphy, B. T. *Black Authors and Illustrators for Children and Young Adults.* 2nd ed. Garland Reference Library of the Humanities. New York: Garland, 1999.

Nilsen, A. P., and K. L. Donelson. *Literature for Today's Young Adults.* 6th ed. New York: Addison-Wesley Longman, 2001.

Outstanding Books for the College Bound: Choices for a Generation. Edited by Marjorie Lewis. Young Adult Library Services Association. Chicago: American Library Association, 1996.

The Reader's Advisor: The Best in Reference Works, British Literature and American Literature. New York: R. R. Bowker, 1921– .

Rochman, Hazel. *Against Borders: Promoting Books for a Multicultural World.* Chicago: Booklist/American Library Association, 1993.

Senior High School Library Catalog. 15th ed. New York: H. W. Wilson, 1997.

Spencer, Pam. *What Do Young Adults Read Next? A Reader's Guide to Fiction for Young Adults.* Detroit: Gale, 1994– .

Top One Hundred Countdown: Best of the Best Books for Young Adults, 1969–1994. Chicago: American Library Association, 1995.

The Young Adult Reader's Advisor. Vol. 1, *The Best in Literature and Language Arts, Mathematics, and Computer Science.* Edited by Myra Immell. New Providence, N.J.: R. R. Bowker, 1992.

Your Reading: A Booklist for Junior High and Middle School Students. Urbana, Ill.: National Council of Teachers of English, published every 3 to 5 years.

Zvirin, Stephanie. *The Best Years of Their Lives: A Resource Guide for Teenagers in Crisis.* 2nd ed. Chicago: American Library Association, 1996.

Selected Recent Books
on Intellectual Freedom

Doyle, R. P. *Banned Books*. Chicago: American Library Association, 2001.

Heins, M. *Not in Front of the Children*. New York: Hill and Wang, 2001.

Intellectual Freedom Manual. 6th ed. Chicago: American Library Association, 2002.

Places I Never Meant to Be: Original Stories by Censored Writers. Edited by Judy Blume. New York: Simon and Schuster, 1999.

Rationales for Challenged Books. Urbana, Ill.: National Council of Teachers of English in partnership with International Reading Association, 1998. Available as a compact disc from the publisher. Originally published as "Rationales for Commonly 'Challenged' Taught Books," edited by D. P. Shugert. *Connecticut English Journal* 15, no. 1 (fall 1983), 145 pp.

Reichman, Henry. *Censorship and Selection: Issues and Answers for Schools*. 3rd ed. Chicago: American Library Association, 2001.

Internet Sites of Intellectual Freedom Advocates

American Booksellers Foundation for Free Expression
   http://www.abffe.org
National Coalition Against Censorship
   http://www.ncac.org
National Council of Teachers of English
   www.ncte.org/censorship
Office for Intellectual Freedom, American Library Association
   http://www.ala.org/alaorg/oif

Note: For an extensive list of First Amendment advocates, visit http://www.ala.org/alaorg/oif/.

Internet Guides to Intellectual Freedom

The following documents are available from the Office for Intellectual Freedom of the American Library Association. More documents are available at http://www.ala.org/alaorg/oif.

Banned Books Week
> http://www.ala.org/bbooks/index.html

Censorship in the Schools: What Is It? How Do You Cope?
> http://www.ala.org/alaorg/oif/censorshipinschools.html

Contacting the Office for Intellectual Freedom Staff plus Other Basic Information
> http://www.ala.org/alaorg/oif/quickoif.html#contact

Coping with Challenges: Kids and Libraries
> http://www.ala.org/alaorg/oif/kidsandlibraries.html

Dealing with Challenges
> http://www.ala.org/alaorg/oif/dealingwithchallenges.html

"The Freedom to Read" Statement
> http://www.ala.org/alaorg/oif/freeread.html

Library Bill of Rights
> http://www.ala.org/work/freedom/lbr.html

Reporting a Challenge
> http://www.ala.org/alaorg/oif/reporting.html

Workbook for Selection Policy Writing
> http://www.ala.org/alaorg/oif/workbook_selection.html

Tips for Dealing with Censorship and Selection

When faced with a book challenge, librarians, teachers, and administrators need immediate, dependable, and practical information about intellectual freedom. One essential source of information is Henry Reichman, *Censorship and Selection: Issues and Answers for Schools,* 3rd ed. (Chicago: American Library Association, 2001). The following are some tips for dealing with censorship and the selection of school materials using Reichman's book:

1. Understand censorship. Read chapter 1, "Censorship in the Schools."

2. Be aware of today's controversial issues. Read chapter 3, "Issues in Dispute."

3. Prepare a selection policy if you don't already have one in place. Read chapter 4, "Establishing Selection Policies."

4. Don't panic! Read chapter 5, "What Do We Do If . . . ?"

5. Understand the law. Read chapter 6, "What Is the Law?"

6. Follow informed procedures. Read chapter 7, "School System Checklist."

7. Have access to basic intellectual freedom documents. Read and study the appendixes, which include the following: "Access to Resources and Services in the School Library Media Program," "Free Access to Libraries for Minors," "Diversity in Collection Development," "Workbook for Selection Policy Writing," "Sample Selection Policy," "Dealing with Concerns about Library Resources," and "Summaries of Selected Legal Cases."

How to Write a Book Rationale

"Be prepared" is the motto of the Boy Scouts. Advocates of literature for young adults should also be prepared before censorship challenges arise. One method of preparing in advance is to create rationales for any materials which have a history of challenges and for any new materials which might be challenged in the future.

What Is a Rationale? What Are Its Components?

Basically, a rationale is a document which outlines the content of the material, discusses the usefulness of the content to the reader or educator, lists awards and accolades the material has won, lists reviews of the work, notes potential objections to the material, and finally offers alternative titles to the work. A rationale thus contains the following components:

Summary of content

Use of content in educational setting or as recreational reading

Awards and honors won by the book

Reviews of the book

Potential objections to the book

Alternative works which might be read in place of this book

How Can the Rationale Be Used?

The rationale serves several purposes. First and foremost, it gathers together in a single document materials which may become important in the event of a challenge. It alerts educators, administrators, parents, students, and librarians to the potential for challenges and provides some immediate ammunition in the event such a challenge occurs.

A Sample Rationale

Title	*The Chocolate War*
Author	Robert Cormier
Publisher	Pantheon
Year of Publication	1974

Book to Be Used for (check all that apply)
- ❑ classroom study
- ❑ recreational reading selection
- ❑ outside reading assignment

Annotation of the Contents

Jerry Renault finds himself embroiled in controversy when, at the direction of the leader of the Vigils, he refuses to sell chocolates in his school's annual fundraising activity. Even after he is instructed to relent and sell the candy, Jerry steadfastly refuses, placing him in opposition to Archie and the entire Vigil gang.

Honors and Awards

ALAN Award, 1983

Best of the Best Books for Young Adults, 1970–1983

Lewis Carroll Shelf Award, 1979

Margaret A. Edwards Award, 1991

Nothin' But the Best: Best of the Best Books for Young Adults, 1966–1986

100 All-Star Choices for Teens, 2000

Still Alive: The Best of the Best Books for Young Adults, 1960–1974

Reviews of the Book

American Libraries 130 (October 1974): 492.

Booklist 71 (March 15, 1975): 747.

English Journal 62 (January 1975): 112.

Horn Book 55 (April 1979): 217.

Kirkus Reviews 42 (April 1974): 371.

Library Journal 99 (May 1974): 1450.

New York Times Book Review, May 5, 1974, p. 15.

Publishers Weekly 205 (April 15, 1974): 52.

School Library Journal 29 (November 1982): 35.

Potential Objections

Several areas of objection have been noted in past challenges. They include inappropriate language, violent scenes, pessimistic ending, sexual content (including masturbation), and religious imagery.

Alternative Reading Selections

Depending upon the nature of the assignment, there are several alternative selections which might be recommended:

Behind the Hidden Door by Rosemary Wells

The Outsiders by S. E. Hinton

The Revelation of St. Bruce by Tres Seymour

Library Bill of Rights

The American Library Association affirms that all libraries are forums for information and ideas, and that the following basic policies should guide their services.

I. Books and other library resources should be provided for the interest, information, and enlightenment of all people of the community the library serves. Materials should not be excluded because of the origin, background, or views of those contributing to their creation.

II. Libraries should provide materials and information presenting all points of view on current and historical issues. Materials should not be proscribed or removed because of partisan or doctrinal disapproval.

III. Libraries should challenge censorship in the fulfillment of their responsibility to provide information and enlightenment.

IV. Libraries should cooperate with all persons and groups concerned with resisting abridgment of free expression and free access to ideas.

V. A person's right to use a library should not be denied or abridged because of origin, age, background, or views.

VI. Libraries which make exhibit spaces and meeting rooms available to the public they serve should make such facilities available on an equitable basis, regardless of the beliefs or affiliations of individuals or groups requesting their use.

Adopted June 18, 1948.
Amended February 2, 1961, and January 23, 1980,
inclusion of "age" reaffirmed January 23, 1996,
by the ALA Council.

The Freedom to Read

An open letter to the citizens of our country from
the National Council of Teachers of English

> *Where suspicion fills the air and holds scholars in line for fear of their
> jobs, there can be no exercise of the free intellect. . . . A problem can no
> longer be pursued with impunity to its edges. Fear stalks the classroom.
> The teacher is no longer a stimulant to adventurous thinking; she becomes
> instead a pipe line for safe and sound information. A deadening dogma
> takes the place of free inquiry. Instruction tends to become sterile; pursuit
> of knowledge is discouraged; discussion often leaves off where it should
> begin.*
>
> —Justice William O. Douglas,
> United States Supreme Court:
> *Adler v. Board of Education,* 1951

The right to read, like all rights guaranteed or implied within our constitutional
tradition, can be used wisely or foolishly. In many ways, education is an effort
to improve the quality of choices open to all students. But to deny the freedom
of choice in fear that it may be unwisely used is to destroy the freedom itself.
For this reason, we respect the right of individuals to be selective in their own
reading. But for the same reason, we oppose efforts of individuals or groups to
limit the freedom of choice of others or to impose their own standards or tastes
upon the community at large.

The right of any individual not just to read but to read whatever he or she
wants to read is basic to a democratic society. This right is based on an assump-
tion that the educated possess judgment and understanding and can be trusted
with the determination of their own actions. In effect, the reader is freed from
the bonds of chance. The reader is not limited by birth, geographic location, or
time, since reading allows meeting people, debating philosophies, and experi-
encing events far beyond the narrow confines of an individual's own existence.

In selecting books for reading by young people, English teachers consider the
contribution which each work may make to the education of the reader, its aesthetic value, its honesty, its readability for a particular group of students, and
its appeal to adolescents. English teachers, however, may use different works for
different purposes. The criteria for choosing a work to be read by an entire
class are somewhat different from the criteria for choosing works to be read by
small groups. For example, a teacher might select John Knowles' *A Separate*

Peace for reading by an entire class, partly because the book has received wide critical recognition, partly because it is relatively short and will keep the attention of many slow readers, and partly because it has proved popular with many students of widely differing abilities. The same teacher, faced with the responsibility of choosing or recommending books for several small groups of students, might select or recommend books as different as Nathaniel Hawthorne's *The Scarlet Letter,* Jack Schaefer's *Shane,* Alexander Solzhenitsyn's *One Day in the Life of Ivan Denisovitch,* Pierre Boulle's *The Bridge over the River Kwai,* Charles Dickens' *Great Expectations,* or Paul Zindel's *The Pigman,* depending upon the abilities and interests of the students in each group. And the criteria for suggesting books to individuals or for recommending something worth reading for a student who casually stops by after class are different from selecting material for a class or group. But the teacher selects, not censors, books. Selection implies that a teacher is free to choose this or that work, depending upon the purpose to be achieved and the student or class in question, but a book selected this year may be ignored next year, and the reverse. Censorship implies that certain works are not open to selection, this year or any year.

Wallace Stevens once wrote, "Literature is the better part of life. To this it seems inevitably necessary to add, provided life is the better part of literature." Students and parents have the right to demand that education today keep students in touch with the reality of the world outside the classroom. Much of classic literature asks questions as valid and significant today as when the literature first appeared, questions like "What is the nature of humanity?" "Why do people praise individuality and practice conformity?" "What do people need for a good life?" and "What is the nature of the good person?" But youth is the age of revolt. To pretend otherwise is to ignore a reality made clear to young people and adults alike on television and radio, in newspapers and magazines. English teachers must be free to employ books, classic or contemporary, which do not lie to the young about the perilous but wondrous times we live in, books which talk of the fears, hopes, joys, and frustrations people experience, books about people not only as they are but as they can be. English teachers forced through the pressures of censorship to use only safe or antiseptic works are placed in the morally and intellectually untenable position of lying to their students about the nature and condition of mankind.

The teacher must exercise care to select or recommend works for class reading and group discussion. One of the most important responsibilities of the English teacher is developing rapport and respect among students. Respect for the uniqueness and potential of the individual, an important facet of the study of literature, should be emphasized in the English class. Literature classes should reflect the cultural contributions of many minority groups in the United States, just as they should acquaint students with contributions from the peoples of Asia.

Rosemary Chance is an assistant professor in the School of Library and Information Science at the University of Southern Mississippi in Hattiesburg, where she teaches graduate and undergraduate classes in children's and young adult literature. She also directs the annual Children's Book Festival, which is in its thirty-fifth year. Her primary research area is literary analysis of Young Adults' Choices novels. She was formerly a public school teacher and school librarian in Texas and Kansas.

Teri S. Lesesne is an associate professor in the department of library science at Sam Houston State University in Huntsville, Tex., where she teaches classes in children's and young adult literature. She is the co-editor of the current edition of *Books for You,* published by the NCTE. Lesesne is a past president of the Texas Council of Teachers of English and has served as the chair of the YALSA Publications Committee. She is the 2002 winner of the Frances Henne/VOYA/YALSA Grant. She writes the young adult review column for *Voices from the Middle* and an author interview column for *Teacher Librarian.*